Ken Davis

LIGHTEN UP!

Great stories from one of America's favorite storytellers

Books by Ken Davis

How to Live with Your Parents Without Losing Your Mind, Zondervan
I Don't Remember Dropping the Skunk, But I Do Remember Trying to Breathe, Zondervan
Fire Up Your Life, Zondervan
Jumper Fables, Zondervan
How to Speak to Youth ... and Keep Them Awake at the Same Time, Zondervan
Lighten Up! Zondervan
Lighten Up! audio, Zondervan
How to Live with Your Kids When You've Already Lost Your Mind, Ken Davis Productions
Secrets of Dynamic Communication, Ken Davis Productions

Find all of Ken's comedy videos, audios, and other resources at www.kendavis.com or Ken Davis Productions, P.O. Box 745940, Arvada, CO 80006-5940, (303) 425-1319.

Ken Davis

LIGHTEN UP!

Great stories from one of America's favorite storytellers

ZondervanPublishingHouse
Grand Rapids, Michigan

A Division of HarperCollinsPublishers

Lighten Up!
Copyright © 2000 by Ken Davis

Requests for information should be addressed to:

ZondervanPublishingHouse
Grand Rapids, Michigan 49530

Library of Congress Cataloging-in-Publication Data

Davis, Ken, 1946-
   Lighten Up! Great Stories from One of America's Favorite Storytellers / Ken Davis.
      p.   cm.
   ISBN 0-310-22757-7 (pbk.)
   1. Christian life—Humor. 2. Christian life—Anecdotes. I. Title.
BV4517.D375 2000
248.4 21—dc21   99-39361
                                                                                  CIP

Published in association with Wolgemuth and Associates, Inc., 330 Franklin Road #135A-106, Brentwood, TN 37027.

Interior design by Korina L. Kelley

Printed in the United States of America

00 01 02 03 04 05 /v DC/ 10 9 8 7 6 5 4 3 2

To my wife, Diane,
who brightens every day
of my life.

Acknowledgments

I would like to thank my family for putting up with me as I spent hours hunched over a computer working on this manuscript. Most of them were very patient. Those who weren't, you know who you are. I love you.

A special thanks to Rob Suggs, whose weird mind and editing skills added so much to this book.

Finally, I want to thank the wonderful, real people who continue to impact my life on a daily basis. These are their stories too. It is their lives that inspire me to lighten up and live.

Contents

Part 1: Living Light

No Easy Steps Foreword 13

Turn Left at the Pink Flamingo 17

The Executioner's Song 20

Things That Go Bump in the Night..........................23

The Old Man in the Mirror 26

Showers of Blessings, Coals of Fire 29

Words That Change Lives 31

Sink Your Teeth into This 34

Here Today, Gone Tomorrow 36

Making a Big "To Do" Out of Life 39

Absolutely Flabulous..41

Who's in Control? 45

Slow Down and Enjoy the Ride....................................49

It's All Downhill from Here 51

Another Night with the Frogs 54

Burned Bridges and Strawberry Underwear 57

Who Holds Tomorrow? 60

Out of Habit...63

Ordinary People, Extraordinary Wisdom 66

"He's Baaaaaack!"...69

I'll Sing for You, Daddy 71

The Author of Joy 74

A Shelter in the Time of Storm 77

Empty Nest 81

Say What You Mean and Mean What You Say.........83

Rest in Peace 87

My Hero 91

Signs of the Times 95

Is Sex a Four-Letter Word? 98

It's Easy! 101

Hit It Straight—Finish Well 104

Alive and Screaming Clean 107

Don't Give Up 110

Part 2: Living Lite

Air Bags, Seat Belts, and Change 115
Opportunity Knocks . . . But Not Always at the Front Door 119
Love in a Vacuum 122
Going First Class 126
Wake Up and Live! 129
The Proof Is in the Tapioca Pudding 132
Bettin' Fifty Bucks on the Lord's Prayer...136
Take It, Stupid! 138
I Wanna Sing! 141
Best Friends 144
You Can't Get There by Standing Here 147
A Dozen Wilted Roses 149
And If I Die Before I Wake...152
Getting Taken for a Ride 156
The Brass Monkey Principle 159
Getting in Character 162
Get on Your Trike and Ride 165
The Three Greatest Words on the Face of the Earth 168
A Story Worth Telling 172
No News Is Bad News 175
No Pain, No Gain...177
The Truth About Cats and Dogs 181
Who Am I?..184
God's Wife 187
What If the Dog Had Been Sitting There? 189
Rump Roast 194
"I've Lost My Father"..196
What Do You Say to God? 199
The Invisible Sweater..202
I See a Ducky and a Horsey 206
Falling in Love Again...210
Ralph and the Nine Nasties 213
The Right Place at the Right Time 216
How to Kill a Grizzly Bear 220
Show Me the Miracle! 224
Leave It There 226

Part 1: Living Light

When Jesus spoke again to the people, he said, "I am the light of the world. Whoever follows me will never walk in darkness, but will have the light of life."   —John 8:12

No Easy Steps Foreword

I set out to write a book just for you. It's filled with real stories about real people. As you read I'm sure you will recognize some places where details have been added or exaggerated to make the reading more fun, and occasionally names have been changed to protect the privacy of people involved.

I want this book to provide genuine hope and encouragement for your life. I hope you'll spit coffee across the room as you laugh at the truth on these pages. I also hope you'll occasionally reach for a tissue to wipe a cleansing tear from your eyes. And it could be that every now and then, you'll spit coffee into the tissue as you laugh and cry simultaneously. So sit back, relax, and enjoy your reading. The lessons drawn from each story still hold the power to jolt your life. Most of all, I hope these stories will lighten your load and brighten your day.

I spent much of my life trying unsuccessfully to live up to unrealistic expectations—and pretending I'd already achieved them. The whole thing left me wading in guilt and totally confused. Was I the only one struggling with the process of becoming everything God created me to be? Everyone else seemed to have it all together. Even my friends maintained the perception of perfection.

Then, every once in a while, someone would come clean. And their moments of honesty were never discouraging. They were never the pity-party, misery-loves-company, muck-wading experiences you might expect. Instead, they were a refreshing affirmation of some important truths. I was *not* an aberration of nature. Life was actually a process for other human beings as well as for me.

It was also wonderful to realize that God is at work in the lives of imperfect people. Hope is the end result of seeing people be honest about their lives. If God cares about imperfect people, then he cares about me. What an encouragement to discover he has the power and he'll help me change— one step at a time. This process of change can only begin as we let people into our lives—as I'll be letting you into my life in the book you're holding.

My friend Carol Maxwell tells about an encounter she had with an intoxicated friend. Carol was seeking to build solid relationships. She'd grown tired of superficial conversations and surface friendships. One night at a party, a bleary-eyed acquaintance ambled up, drink in hand, and inquired, "How are you doing?" Then, without waiting for Carol's answer, the woman turned and waved at someone across the room.

The insincerity was too much. Instead of responding in kind, Carol rebelled. She smiled and replied, in normal conversational cadence, "Hey, diddle diddle. The cat and the fiddle. The cow jumped over the moon."

Her acquaintance noticed nothing irregular. She wasn't even listening. As Carol finished, the woman touched her arm gently and responded, "How nice!" Then she set off for another corner, another face, another meaningless conversation.

Mother Goose? Why not? Carol could have offered a full confession to murdering her husband and spooning him into the garbage disposal. She would have received the same reply—"How nice!" Yes, I know that people with dulled senses make easy targets; yet we're all victims of the same social disconnection. Why do we seem to lack the time or courage to connect meaningfully with those around us?

Try this simple test. Hang out in the lobby of your church one Sunday. You're likely to meet someone like Bill Jones, who's struggling to keep his life together. As his marriage crumbles, he's drifting into an affair. Bill stands at one of those great crossroads in life. What he needs is someone to help him put his life in perspective—to warn him of the treacherous cliff he's approaching.

As people mill about in their Sunday best, Samuel Carter steps forward. Samuel has just been laid off and his daughter has been expelled from school for using drugs. "How's it going, Bill?" Samuel asks, a broad smile and a firm handshake obscuring his insecurity and fear.

"Things are great," Bill lies. "How about for you?"

"Same old grind," Samuel responds. He doesn't hint at the depth and pain of that grind. He simply puts in a moment or two of small talk punctuated by his best wishes. Then two men who desperately need each other go their separate ways, never connecting.

I remember attending a horrible party. A broken heart makes any celebration intolerable, and I didn't want to be there. I was in a room full of strangers, and I was hurting as badly as I'd ever hurt in my life.

I was relieved to see the face of a friend who I knew would have a sympathetic ear. He spotted me too and began to make his way toward me through the crowd.

My life was a mess, and I desperately needed encouragement. I needed a foothold so I could begin to climb out of the terrible pit I was in. "It's so good to see you," I said, embracing my friend and clasping his hand firmly in mine. "How are you?"

"If I were any better, I'd be twins," he bubbled.

My heart tipped up on end and began to sink like the Titanic. I was falling to pieces and my soul was in shreds. My spirit didn't have enough substance to be a shadow. How could I relate to someone so on top of things that he'd cloned himself into twins? I knew there'd be no healing that night.

"How 'bout you?" he inquired.

"Never been better," I lied.

Several days later I caught my friend alone. This time I dared to pour out my soul, and he was indeed a friend. He listened, he cried, and he prayed with me. He also told me the truth. His bubbly exterior at the party had been a trick done with smoke and mirrors. Behind the cheerful, not-a-care-in-the-world exterior, he too was struggling. The twins were gone; he became an only child again.

In the midst of pretending, we'd almost missed each other.

What kept us from making that connection is the same thing that kept Carol and her friend, as well as the men in church, from moving more deeply into each other's lives. It is our reluctance to be honest. "Never let them see you sweat," the deodorant advertisement proclaims. That may be good advice for underarms, but it's dreadfully bad advice for the heart.

During this difficult time in my life, I remember reading a book by a well-known author, Mr. Perfect (not his real name). Mr. Perfect had written a book titled *Six Simple Steps to Having It All Together Like I Do* (not the real name of the book). The more I read, the more I felt like a failure. This man was the epitome of what I wanted to be. The accounts of his family, his faith, and his success were spotless. There were no arguments with his wife, no temptations that weren't immediately conquered with a brief but eloquent prayer.

Part of me wanted to gag, but the other parts (I told you I was falling apart) latched on to the possibility that such a perfect life was possible. The result was not hope, but a movement toward guilt and despair. The only ray of hope came from the fact that none of the parts of me had ever actually met such a person.

I have an opinion about those who make claims that any aspect of life can be conquered by following easy steps: They should be hog-tied and dragged up and down those steps until they finally shout the truth: "Life isn't that easy!" If this sounds vindictive, please understand that I believe this revenge should be taken with the utmost of Christian kindness.

Almost a month to the day after I stopped reading Mr. Perfect's book, he came to a sad public disgrace. I took no pleasure in his fall, but I did take the facts as Exhibit A in a lifelong parade of evidence leading to a single truth: There are no perfect people.

The book you are reading was not written by Mr. Perfect. It was written by Ken Davis, a sinner wonderfully saved by grace. If you are still in-process, if you face real problems in your everyday life, then this book is for you. If you lose your temper, fall short of your goals, make honest mistakes, and sometimes commit intentional sins, keep turning the pages. There is hope for change. Enjoy the laughter and insight in these stories.

Lighten up and live!

Turn Left at the Pink Flamingo

My sister Carol's directions to her house seemed simple enough:

Go east on 494 to Highway 52.

Take 52 South to the big sign reading Douglas Trail Road. You can't miss it.

Go east on Douglas Trail until it comes to an end—that'll be Highway 36.

Go south on 36 until you see a huge pink flamingo standing beside the road.

Take the next left. From there, we're just a few miles down the road on your left.

I missed three clues that this would be one long trip.

Clue Number One was the map provided by the rental car agency. One side of the map showed a detailed representation of every street, alley, and bike path within a one-mile radius of the agency. For each house there was a square—with a tiny little picture of the family who lived there. Much as I enjoyed seeing which lawns currently needed cutting and who had the coolest toolsheds, none of it was too helpful for driving halfway across the state.

The other side of the map depicted the entire world. A map of this scale couldn't be bothered with cities populated by fewer than two million people or highways with fewer than six lanes. I needed the magnifying glass to spot the 150 miles on my route. The words "Douglas Trail Road" did not appear on this map. No pink flamingos were in sight. On the other hand, it was the first road map I'd ever seen that included the edge of Mars.

Clue Number Two was the mantra, "You can't miss it." Sorry—I'm fully capable of missing six overturned semis that spilled Jell-O across the New Jersey Turnpike. Once, when I was driving to Minnesota from Colorado, a single wrong turn took me 180 miles into Kansas. I missed the huge sign at the border that said, "Welcome to Kansas." Dorothy, Toto, and several dozen flying monkeys made no impression on me.

As you might expect, I also missed the turn for Douglas Trail Road. There are actually three signs on Highway 52 that bear the words "Douglas Trail." The last of these was, in fact, the correct turn, but Carol had apparently not considered this a worthwhile travel tip. She must have figured I'd be guided by some interior Carol-seeking radar system.

Wrong again. The first time I saw the word "Douglas," I took the bait. I even called on my cell phone to confirm that "Douglas" was the name I was looking for. "You're almost here!" my sister giggled excitedly. "I can hardly wait to see you."

I was not almost there, and she would be waiting quite a long time to see me. This particular Douglas Road wound its way through vast, gaping expanses of Minnesota farmland with no sign of human life—only herds of black-and-white cattle. I had set off on a voyage where no man had gone before. Judging by the look on the faces of the rheumy-eyed cows that watched me pass, it was obvious that few cars ever ventured this way. The theme song for "The Twilight Zone" began ringing in my head.

It bothered me when the cows stopped chewing as I went by. They were discreet about it, but their heads slowly swiveled as their eyes followed my car. Even when they'd shrunk to a tiny dot in my rearview mirror, they were still looking my way, ruminating—their dull, bovine minds trying to find a way to break it to me that I was not on Douglas Trail Road.

Finally, after almost an hour of driving, the road ended. But the intersecting road was not Highway 56; it was Highway 12. The helpful map showed that I was still somewhere in the United States, perhaps in a section of the Louisiana Purchase. I reached for the cell phone again. I called Carol—long distance—and acknowledged that I was lost. She said, "Ask directions from someone on the corner." I looked up and down the road; I could see for miles. There were only acres of corn, a weathered oak tree, and one black-and-white cow.

The cow wasn't talking. I retraced my route and finally found the right Douglas Trail Road.

I should have caught the final clue that this was going to be a long trip. It was the instruction to turn at the sight of a huge pink flamingo by the side of the road. Let me leave you with this travel tip of my own:

Never, ever use a living thing as a landmark for giving directions. Living things move. I suppose I should have known that it wasn't a real flamingo. Highway 52 connects Minneapolis and Rochester, Minnesota. Flamingos live and flourish in warm states like Florida. You can see hundreds of them at Sea World standing on one foot and reminiscing about the Jurassic Period, before the Ice Age, when they used to live in Minnesota. That's why they stand on one foot. They're still trying to get the other one warm.

I never found the flamingo. The state police helped me find my sister.

The old saying "All roads lead to Rome" is not true. Douglas Road doesn't lead to Rome, Albuquerque, or anyplace else. It leads to one nonspeaking black-and-white cow.

If you want to get somewhere, you have to know where you're going. Then you must plan how to get there. There are many people seeking God who are on their own personal Douglas Roads. Jesus gave simple and perfect directions to finding God—no flamingos, no detours, and no bad maps.

Jesus answered, "I am the way and the truth and the life. No one comes to the Father except through me." —*John 14:6*

The Executioner's Song

Ken was still seventeen years old when he enlisted in the army. He was one of twelve children, and he recognized his chance to make something of himself. He couldn't have known the United States would be at war within a matter of months.

At eighteen, Ken found himself in the thick of battle defending the Philippines against the onslaught of a Japanese attack. One day he lay behind a log and watched as enemy soldiers overran his position by the hundreds. Ken and a companion hid their rifles and surrendered. It marked the beginning of a three-and-a-half year nightmare. Ken became a prisoner of war.

The grim realities of prison camp quickly decimated Ken's health. He'd survived the grueling Bataan death march only to be wracked with malaria and dysentery. In prison camp, the privilege of remaining alive depended on a prisoner's ability to work. Those who were gravely ill or incapable of labor were shot or perhaps buried alive. The young man's weight dropped below one hundred pounds, but he struggled to make himself useful enough to avoid execution. It was no good; frail as he was, Ken was fighting a losing battle.

The war drew to a close, and Japanese defeat became a looming certainty. As the captors' prospects dwindled, their atrocities increased in number and intensity. The Japanese began executing prisoners at random.

One day, Ken found himself lying beneath the thatch roof of a hut with several other prisoners. As a Japanese officer shouted commands from the hut's balcony, prisoners were dragged from the shelter in pairs to a nearby rice paddy. The bonds were cut from their hands, and they were summarily bayoneted to death or shot in the head.

Ken watched his friends dying two by two, knowing his time would come. As evening approached, the shrill voice of the Japanese officer shouted yet another command. Ken and his friend were wrenched from the hut and dragged into the rice paddy. Kneeling in the mud, he waited in terror for the inevitable. There was another shout from the hut—then an explosion in his head. Ken fell forward into the filthy water.

He hadn't been shot. He'd been struck with the butt of a rifle. The sun had gone down, and the Japanese didn't conduct executions after sundown. As he regained his senses, Ken knew this would be his last night on earth. As sure as the sun would rise in the morning, the executions would continue.

Huddled sleeplessly that night, Ken's life flashed before him. He saw the face of his mother. He recalled the admonitions of his father, a stern Nazarene evangelist. He thought of his brothers, some of them fighting for their country in theaters of war across Europe. Ken whispered his farewells.

He also remembered his sins. Every sin he'd committed, from minor indiscretion to shameful transgression, flashed before his eyes. Yet his guilt gave way. It vanished in a great wave of peace that rose up and flooded Ken's soul. The faith he'd placed in Jesus Christ years ago, as a small boy, was suddenly present and potent. He was reminded of the price paid for each of those sins. He was forgiven.

By the time Ken watched the sun rise, a miracle had taken place. Facing certain death, he felt no fear. He'd made his peace with God, and he was emotionally overwhelmed with the reality of grace and forgiveness.

The cool silence of dawn was shattered by the call of the executioner. Ken heard the approaching boots of the guards. They yanked him to his feet—then led him back to the prison sector.

The executions had halted.

Ken would live to return from one of history's bloodiest conflicts—if just barely. On the day of liberation, he was little more than a skeleton. Desperately sick and half-starved, he weighed eighty-five pounds. He was so weak that he needed assistance to clear a two-inch board at the back of the truck bound for freedom.

This is a story I know by heart. Its hero is my father, Ken Davis Sr. And the most amazing element of the entire narrative is the placing of his emphasis in its telling. He focuses not on God saving him from the bayonets and bullets of enemy soldiers, but on God saving him from his sin. If God could forgive the sins that paraded before him that dark night, then not even the razor edge of a bayonet, or the brutal impact of a bullet, could separate him from that love.

My father had endured considerable physical abuse; malnutrition and malaria had taken their toll. The medics examined my father and concluded he would not live to old age. Certainly, they told him, he couldn't have children

That was more than half a century ago. They underestimated my dad. He's seventy-five years old now, and I'm one of the five children they said he couldn't have. I cling to one lesson from the fascinating stories of Dad's POW experience: In those dark, horrible moments when death confronted him, my dad had an authentic supernatural encounter with grace. Peace overcame him; fear was driven out.

Just a thought:

Years after my dad's experience, I would face my own moment of hopeless desperation. The situation would be different, but I faced the same ultimate enemy. The same guilty review of sins would play back in an endless loop. The possible consequences would be the same, too.

Yet the same liberation that freed my father broke my shackles too. And trusting in God's unconditional forgiveness and love can bring the same peace to you—no matter what enemy, no matter what battle, no matter what sin seeks to destroy you.

Who shall separate us from the love of Christ? Shall trouble or hardship or persecution or famine or nakedness or danger or sword? As it is written: "For your sake we face death all day long; we are considered as sheep to be slaughtered." No, in all these things we are more than conquerors through him who loved us. For I am convinced that neither death nor life, neither angels nor demons, neither the present nor the future, nor any powers, neither height nor depth, nor anything else in all creation, will be able to separate us from the love of God that is in Christ Jesus our Lord. —Romans 8:35–39

Things That Go Bump in the Night

My wife Diane is not okay.

A few nights ago, she woke me from a sound sleep. "Listen!" she whispered in a terrified voice. I was instantly awake. I couldn't get my eyes open wide enough to see in the dark. "There it is again," she hissed.

My heart was pounding. I still couldn't see, but I was trying. My eyes bulged outward as if that might help me see in the dark. I was waiting for the gun to go off or the ax to fall.

"It's in the garage," she said, squeezing my arm so hard the blood ceased to flow to my fingers. Several times I tried to get her to give me more information. "Shhhhh!" she interrupted. "What if he escaped from somewhere?"

Now she was letting her imagination run wild. "What if he has a chain saw?" she gasped. The fingers on my left hand were now cold and blue. Suddenly, with a violent little shove, she pushed me out of bed with a command: "Go see."

"Let me see if I have this right," I whispered back. "You think there's someone in the garage?"

"Yes," she answered. "I heard the noise."

"And you think he escaped from somewhere," I confirmed.

"Yes—what if he escaped from one of those crazy places?" she whimpered.

"And you're fairly certain he has a chain saw."

"Yes! Like in those horror movies! What if he's planning to cut us up?"

"And you want me to confront him," I growled, "in my Fruit of the Loom underwear?"

How effective could I possibly be? I could just see myself standing in my underwear facing some burly psycho waving a chain saw. "Hey, you!" I'd shout. "Take your chain saw and get out of here!" If he didn't respond, what would I do—scare him by snapping the elastic on my shorts?

Perhaps you think I'm being unfair to Diane. Not so. I'm being more than fair. She is not okay, and I love her that way. I'm convinced that one of the reasons we've been married for over thirty years is because we're free to laugh with each other about these things.

Diane has never asked me to stop telling any story I've shared with audiences over the years. There are stories I've chosen not to tell, but this isn't one of them. Hundreds of men and women have told me of similar experiences in their homes.

I shared the chain-saw story with a large audience one evening. Returning to my seat, I found Diane laughing uncontrollably. "What has gotten into you?" I asked.

"I was just thinking," she choked. "I've seen your underwear. I think you *could* hold off a man with a chain saw." Touché!

After a year of marriage I lost track of how much sleep I lost after waking to the words, "Did you hear that?" It always turned out to be a romantic cat prowling beneath the bedroom window, or a pet that was accidentally locked in the garage. Never once was it a guy with a chain saw.

All negative emotions loom larger in the dark. Problems invariably seem bleaker. I'll lie awake thinking about a book deadline or a personal problem. The darkness amplifies the issue until it seems insurmountable. Guilt and fear thrive in darkness.

But the dawn brings us new hope and a brighter outlook. The chain-saw stalker now strikes us as amusing. Nightmares and other bumps in the night lose their power in the fresh morning light, and the accuser slinks away. Darkness magnifies evil and provides an ideal setting for negative thinking. If we fear the dark, why not seek the light?

A woman once stood before Jesus in the midst of a real-life nightmare. Her attackers held no chain saws; they held stones. They'd caught her in the act of adultery and were prepared to hurl rocks at her until her body was lifeless. She stood helpless, terrified, and guilty. The law demanded a violent execution by stoning. Darkness had overwhelmed any light that might ever have shined in her life. All was discovered; all was hopeless:

> *The teachers of the law and the Pharisees brought in a woman caught in adultery. They made her stand before the group and said to Jesus, "Teacher, this woman was caught in the act of adultery. In the Law Moses commanded us to stone such women. Now what do you say?"* —John 8:3–5

In the midst of this darkness and terror—as the gaping doors of hell widened before her—a blinding ray of hope suddenly burst on the scene. It was the light of grace and forgiveness, in the form of a man—a man unlike any other she had ever met. It was Jesus Christ who faced her accusers.

The men pelted Jesus not with stones but with questions. He finally straightened up and threw back a simple challenge:

> *If any one of you is without sin, let him be the first to throw a stone at her.* —John 8:7

The ray of hope intensified, its warmth banishing the monsters of the night:

> *At this, those who heard began to go away one at a time, the older ones first, until only Jesus was left, with the woman still standing there. Jesus straightened up and asked her, "Woman, where are they? Has no one condemned you?"*
>
> *"No one, sir," she said.*
>
> *"Then neither do I condemn you," Jesus declared. "Go now and leave your life of sin."* —John 8:9–11

Only moments earlier, this woman had faced death. Now, in the brightness of love and forgiveness, a new life seemed more than possible. She could see into all the dark corners; the terror of the night was gone.

Just a thought:

If you find yourself making decisions in the dark; if you find yourself living in the grip of guilt; or if you find yourself in your underwear facing chain saws—it's time to move into the light. After the woman's accusers had dropped their stones and walked away, and after the woman had experienced cleansing forgiveness and a new lease on life, the very next words from Jesus' mouth were these:

> *I am the light of the world. Whoever follows me will never walk in darkness, but will have the light of life.* —John 8:12

The Old Man in the Mirror

Ten years had passed since I'd seen this cast of characters. Here were most of my old classmates. Here were a good number of my old teachers too. And here I was—astounded by how much everybody else had aged. A high-school reunion is a strange and frightening experience.

My vibrant young classmates had remained forever sixteen in my mental archives. My memories of them certainly didn't match the aging museum pieces exhibited before me. Crew-cuts had given way to shiny radar domes. Former baby faces were now creased with crow's-feet. Young, firm bodies had sagged into middle-age play dough.

We were no longer puppies—we were dogs. We had studied physical phenomena such as gravity and natural erosion; now we were living them. Funny what ten years did to that cute little mole that embellished the smile on my dream girl's face. Now I understood the phrase, "making a mountain out of a molehill." No two ways about it: Ten years of natural devastation were staring me in the face. I had real sympathy for these poor souls.

That's when the unthinkable occurred to me. Could it possibly be that I, too, had suffered the ravages of time? I ran into the locker room to scrutinize my own face. Could I conceivably look as old and used-up as my classmates? I didn't feel as if I'd changed so much. As I skidded around the corner into the shower area, I realized that one thing had not changed—the smell of the locker room. That manly aroma still lingered on. I took a deep breath of the air and relived the basketball games, cheap soap, and forever-missing athletic supporters of yore.

Another unidentified odor suggested the disturbing possibility that one supporter-wearer might be mummified in some secret nook of the locker room. My mind flashed back to the day they stuffed Richard Dixon into a locker as a prank. It crossed my mind that I couldn't remember anyone letting him out.

The mirror was in the same place and condition as when I'd last consulted it. There was just enough silver plating left to give me that

"Picasso" look. I found a fragment large enough to depict both eyes on the same head, and I sized myself up. Yes! While all my classmates had aged considerably, I was still as young as the day I graduated.

Still, as I left, I had a lingering suspicion that my classmates didn't see me that way. As a matter of fact, I knew deep down I looked older. But I'd observed the changes in my own appearance gradually, over a period of time. I'd watched it all in slow motion. Car crashes and avalanches are never as frightening that way either.

Some of the brightest students had ended their education on the day of graduation. Others, marginal students when I knew them, had gone on to brilliant careers. A former shrinking violet was now a successful sales director. Mister Self-Confidence of old had telegraphed his insecurity by renting a luxury car to impress people who no longer needed impressing. A beautiful young woman turned out to be the gangly slow-bloomer whom everyone teased years ago. Old flames had stopped smoking entirely. Some classmates had self-destructed, while others had flourished. A few hadn't changed a bit—in their level of maturity, at least.

I had changed dramatically in ten years—no doubt about it. But much of the evidence was diluted as I found myself falling back into old patterns. The old social pecking order may have expired, but in my mind it still held some sort of power. It wasn't until the twenty-year reunion that reality set in. I didn't have to check the locker-room mirror. I knew I looked like everyone else.

At the twenty-year reunion, the attitudes of my classmates were different as well. There were fewer desperate efforts to impress. Most of us were more concerned about family and renewing old friendships than we were about making new impressions. That evening I spent hours talking with people, building deeper friendships than I would ever have felt possible.

How tragic that those friendships never developed in high school. The people I most remember from those years were not the ones who impressed me, but the ones who influenced me for the good—like Mary Ellen, the principal's daughter. She always treated me with kindness and respect. She would always take time to talk and help and smile. I remember Diane Drew, whose infectious laugh and commonsense advice were free to all, regardless of social status.

I remember Roger Gruben, whose athletic ability did not stop him from being the friend of Ken Davis, a person with the hand-eye coordination of a carp.

I'd always looked back on my high-school years as a victim of adolescent cruelty. But after my twentieth reunion, I see it differently. My own feelings of inadequacy and my skewed vision of my place in the world made me a very poor prospect as a friend. I selfishly sought affirmation and offered little in return. A relationship with me was a one-way street going my way.

In many ways I was a victim of my own narrow vision. I bought the false social structure hook, line, and sinker. The whole structure was an illusion. It was so superficial that it dissolved the day we graduated. Yet we endowed it with power that can affect lives years later.

Today it doesn't matter who played on the football team or won a speech contest. It doesn't matter who belonged to what clique. Today I only wish I'd given more. Smiled more. Been more helpful. Reached out to those who could have used my help.

Just a thought:

My class skipped the thirty-year reunion. After I'd written this segment, Linda called—the unpretentious, smiling cheerleader; another friend who accepted me just as I was. She is planning a thirty-fifth reunion and I'm already looking forward to it. It'll be fun to look in the locker-room mirror and see the old guy who looks back. I know something now that I didn't know before. It's something that will make me so much more aware of the others who attend. It will help me to be a better friend. It will keep me from ever again thinking of myself as a hapless victim.

I know this: God loved the skinny little guy I was in high school, and he loves the old guy in the locker-room mirror today.

Look in the mirror. He feels the same about you.

How great is the love the Father has lavished on us, that we should be called children of God! And that is what we are!   —1 John 3:1

Showers of Blessings, Coals of Fire

Jerry had been on my mind all day. Why not pick up the phone and give him a call?

As I dialed his number, Jerry was reaching for his own phone to call me—but he was distraught. He pastors a growing church in a small community. God was blessing his work in many ways, yet now Jerry was facing criticism. And the criticism was very cold, very cruel, and very personal.

Just ahead was a meeting with four disgruntled families from Jerry's congregation. They were planning to leave the church, but not without some parting shots. These folks had some legitimate concerns, to be sure, but the negative spirit and personal nature of their attack would make for a painful meeting. Jerry knew what the accusations would be, and he was preparing his defense. He wasn't operating from a base of conceit or confidence. He was reacting to the pain that unjust criticism brings. In times like these, feelings of inadequacy rush to the forefront; questions of self-worth take hold of us: I wonder if I should even be a pastor—am I a failure?

"What should I do?" Jerry asked me.

I'm the last person on earth qualified to give advice to a pastor. I tried desperately to think of something I could say that would help him in his defense. Then I remembered something. Actually, an old tune began to play in my head: "Showers of Blessings," a song we used to sing when I was a kid.

And along with the tune came a mental image that made me laugh out loud. It was a picture of hurtful, critical, graceless souls—all of them treading water in a sea of blessing and grace. "Rain on them," I blurted out to Jerry. "Deluge them in a sea of love. Where apology is needed, apologize freely. Where unjust criticism is leveled, do not defend yourself.

"Don't try to keep them in the church, Jerry. Pray with them. Pray they'll find a pastor they're comfortable with, a church that uses methods they can agree with, and a youth pastor who never crosses boundaries of propriety. [This was one of their main concerns.]

"Then, Jerry, send them away in a flood of your blessing. The most unjustly criticized and falsely accused man ever to live made no attempt to defend himself. From a bloody cross he showered his executioners with blessings. He cried, 'Forgive them, for they do not know what they are doing.'"

Jerry was overwhelmed with relief as he shook loose the burden of self-defense. He didn't have to endure the agony of presenting an argument he couldn't win. Arguments and defenses never resolve these situations. I've never heard a case of disgruntled people canceling their plans to leave a church because of a pastor's clever defense. No, those efforts only intensify the rift and polarize the players. As I saw it, Jerry had two options:

If there was valid criticism, he needed to listen and learn.

If there were cruel attacks, he needed to drench his accusers in grace and love.

"Showers of blessings? No, make that a deluge of blessings," I said. "After the meeting, when you open your office door, they'll come flying out in a torrent of water. It will look like a scene from the Titanic. They'll be treading water to stay afloat in the torrent. Chances are they'll still seek another church—but they'll never forget that ride. What can their argument be in the face of such a gracious response? 'Don't love me? Don't bless me? Don't let me go with grace?'"

Jerry thanked me for my call and my counsel. I hung up and sat silently for a moment, basking in the brilliant advice I'd just given. The shrill ring of the phone, as well as the equally shrill voice at the other end, startled me. "I ordered one of your videotapes over a month ago, and I still haven't received it! I thought this was a Christian organization. How can you be so sloppy in business and call yourself a Christian?"

So soon: a chance to practice what I preached. I paused, took a deep breath . . . and gave her a piece of my mind.

Just a thought:

Do not take revenge, my friends, but leave room for God's wrath, for it is written: "It is mine to avenge; I will repay," says the Lord. On the contrary: "If your enemy is hungry, feed him; if he is thirsty, give him something to drink. In doing this, you will heap burning coals on his head." —Romans 12:19–20

Words That Change Lives

I sat in a small chair. Across the desk from me sat the formidable Francis W. Peterson.

Mrs. Peterson, as we were instructed to call her, was my English teacher. She was in her fifties and just a slip of a woman. But what she lacked in size, she made up for in her ability to command attention. Mrs. Peterson could effortlessly dominate a class of agitated adolescents who were overdosing on postpubescent hormones.

I had disrupted her attempts to nurture teenage appreciation of Shakespeare. Now I'd pay the ultimate penalty for my actions. I was doing hard time—one hour of sitting absolutely still, without so much as a peep.

The way I saw it, I'd been unjustly convicted. My teacher had cursed. In 1963, neither teachers nor students were permitted to curse within the confines of a school building. But Francis W. Peterson had cursed. I was minding my own business, daydreaming about Linda Gustafson, when I heard my teacher say the "d" word: "Out, out, damned spot!"

She uttered that word without a hint of shame. Her daring creative expression seemed to me to mark the dawning of a new, more permissive era. That's why I suggested to the class further forbidden adjectives Shakespeare might have considered.

Punishment was swift. I knew I'd gone too far, and I was ashamed of my disrespectful attempt at humor. I liked Mrs. Peterson; her no-nonsense approach to teaching couldn't hide the fact that she cared for her students. My better judgment had been clouded by a desire to impress my peers.

Now, as I sat watching her correct papers, I was certain there'd be further sanctions of justice. Mrs. Peterson finished her work. I stared at her long, slender fingers as she capped the pen and folded her hands.

"Kenneth Davis," she said with a voice that demanded eye contact. I raised my eyes from her fingers, and she fixed me with that "you should know better" gaze. Almost imperceptibly, she shook her head and made the dreaded *tsk-tsk* sound. I'd rather have been beaten with a ruler than have heard that sound and been the recipient of that look of disappointment. I waited for the pronouncement. Perhaps it would be banishment from the human race until adulthood. Surely I'd be banished from school.

She caught me totally off guard. "God has given you a gift," she said. "You have a wonderful sense of humor."

Before I could reply, she continued. "You've been using this gift to destroy my class, but that's going to change. I want you to go out for speech."

I didn't want to go out for speech. All my friends wore letter jackets with macho symbols like footballs, baseball bats, and hockey sticks embroidered on the shoulder. I wasn't about to walk around my high school with lips sewn on my jacket. I wanted to be an athlete. It was athletic ability that was rewarded in my social circles. All my life I'd been berated and ostracized because I had no athletic ability. I felt cheated. I was born with a competitive spirit and the coordination of a carp.

Francis W. Peterson persisted. She eventually persuaded me to go out for speech. I won nearly every contest I entered. And that opened doors to a wonderful career. It ultimately allowed me to travel across the world with an opportunity to inspire and encourage millions of people with my words. My speaking, in turn, opened still other doors: I was allowed to write books and appear on stage and television.

The confidence to pursue a unique and wonderful calling was made possible because of one person—a person who saw potential, dared to call it a gift from God, and cared enough to encourage its development. What a revelation! I wasn't just weird; I was weirdly gifted. I'd expected punishment, but instead I had received the wonderful gift of encouragement.

Twenty-five years after my high-school graduation, I met Francis W. Peterson again. I presented her with a bouquet of flowers and a heartfelt thank-you. In a restaurant overlooking the Pacific Ocean, I told her how her encouragement and guidance had changed the course of my life.

I'll never be an athlete. I'll never be an intellectual giant or a great spiritual leader. But because of her love and encouragement, I followed a dream that led to a rich life and a fulfilling career. I'll continue to be the unique and strange person God created me to be. I'll continue to use my gifts to bring truth and encouragement to others, and to help them live to their fullest potential. All of this I'll do because someone dared to proclaim, "God has given you a gift."

Thank you, Mrs. Peterson.

Just a thought:

Words of encouragement change lives. Take a moment to think back on your life. Who was there to encourage you? Was it a parent, a teacher, a coach, a pastor, or church worker? Perhaps it was a total stranger. Sometimes all that is required is a word.

With just six words—"God has given you a gift"—Mrs. Peterson lit a fire of confidence and desire that helped change the course of my life. Learn the discipline of finding opportunities to encourage loved ones and strangers. Don't expect a response or anything else in return. Just do it.

Say the words that change lives.

Sink Your Teeth into This

I love the old "creature features." The classic monster movies were campy, they were corny, and they still managed to be scary—especially the vampire ones. Somehow the filmmakers portrayed a subtle message of hope that is missing in many of the dark, graphic films of today.

Now don't throw the book across the room. I'm not into the occult. Hear me out—then you can throw the book across the room.

First of all, I don't believe there are such things as vampires. Even if there were, they wouldn't be a threat to any person of average intelligence. Anyone could avoid their dental aberration by following just a few simple rules. Stay with me 'til the end now.

Ken's commonsense rules for avoiding vampires:

1. Don't go near the place where vampires live, especially at night. In these corny movies, the most horrific scenes occur when some mentally challenged individual decides to investigate the place where the vampires sleep. No wonder there's such violence! If someone woke you up in the middle of a sound sleep, you'd be snarling too.

2. Give yourself some time! If you foolishly decide to go to the Fang Fortress, go as soon as the sun comes up so you'll have all day to "stake things out." Any nitwit knows the monsters can't do anything when the sun is out. I'll never understand why the people in the movies always go sneaking into the dungeon about fifteen minutes before the sun goes down. Duh!

3. Eat lots of Italian food and keep some extra snacks in your pockets. For some reason, vampires hate garlic. Me, I love garlic. I have such a bad case of garlic breath that I've never even dreamed about a vampire. I think there's a connection. So if you intend to go hunting for the "batman," it might be a good idea to avoid brushing your teeth for several days.

4. Don't sleep.
   (Stay with me now, there's a point to all this. Just trust me and keep going.)

5. If there's a bat fluttering outside your window, don't open the window.
6. Carry a mirror everywhere and don't talk to anyone who doesn't have a reflection.
7. Don't hang around virgins. Vampires always seem to have an unhealthy interest in virgins.
8. Avoid people who hiss.
9. Never go anywhere without a cross.

There's the clincher. In the old vampire movies there's an undeniable power associated with the cross. One person could hold off a horde of vampires simply by lifting up the cross. The flesh of the vampire would burn when it came in contact with the cross. Evil could not conquer in the presence of the cross.

There are no vampires, but every day we all face hissing demons that go for the jugular—demons such as anger, greed, selfishness, temptation, and pride. They flutter constantly at our windows, seeking to cast their spells over our lives. Our first reaction is to grab the torches and storm the castle, chanting, "I'll never do that again ... I'll never talk to my kids like that again ... I'll never give in to that temptation again ... I'm going to be different." Sometimes we are foolish enough to prowl the haunts of the very temptations we fight. In doing so, we break the first rule of avoiding vampires: *Don't go where they live.*

Just a thought:

Many of the rules for avoiding vampires surely apply. But the greatest safety, the greatest effectiveness in fighting your personal vampires, comes from the shadow of the cross. Political clout, legalistic rules, behavior modification, and sin management will eventually fail. What happened on the cross took the sting from the most hideous of evils—death itself.

"Where, O death, is your victory? Where, O death, is your sting?" The sting of death is sin, and the power of sin is the law. But thanks be to God! He gives us the victory through our Lord Jesus Christ.
—*1 Corinthians 15:55–57*

Here Today, Gone Tomorrow

My calendar reads November 1, 1998. Outside, the world is slowly giving way to panic. And what's at the root of this frenzy? Experts say tens of thousands of computers will stop working at the stroke of midnight on the eve of the year 2000.

Many of these computers affect military operations, air traffic control, tax assessments, and social security. Some believe the computers connected to banks and utilities will instantly freeze, creating immediate international chaos. This, as you know, is the Y2K Problem, or the Millennium Bug (not to be confused with the C3PO Problem; that was a Star Wars bug).

The only computer I ever mastered was the Fisher Price 2000 Speak and Spell. Remember that one? You could take it into the bathtub with you. I'm not much of a techno-cyber wizard, but here's a grossly simplistic explanation of what occurred. When computers were first introduced, someone had a nifty idea. They could save precious space in the basic computer code—two whole digits' worth. That's why they frugally used only two digits to designate years, meaning 81 for 1981, 97 for 1997, and so on.

This worked really well, and there was much hearty backslapping and congratulations all around in the Massive Decisions Room—at first. But suddenly, there was a collective gasp. It came out that someone (we won't mention any names, but I promise it wasn't me) forgot all about the millennium, that Big Looming Thing peeking out from under the calendar.

Thus, at the stroke of midnight on December 31, 1999, time-sensitive computers—millions of them—will flip to a 00 indication for the year 2000. Your hard drive, though capable of computing the world's key economic indicators or calculating advanced nuclear physics, will scratch its head and decide the year 1900 has rolled around again. Experts—millions of them—are predicting digital weeping, wailing, and gnashing of circuits.

Forecasts range from minor inconvenience to international catastrophe. Those of you who are reading this book after the crisis—you can fill in the end of the story. Not me. I'm speaking to you from the tail end of 1998, and I have no idea what the actual outcome will be. I do, however, know this:

After midnight of December 31, 1999, nothing will ever be the same.

I can make that prediction with utter confidence. Why? Because it would be true with or without the Y2K crisis. We live as though the status quo is eternal, even as everything around us is constantly changing. Many changes are so gradual we don't notice them—and that's the human element that permitted the Y2K problem to develop in the first place.

Personally, I believe this international media event will wake us up to the simple truth that nothing on earth is permanent. The only constant is change. That's a lesson we stubbornly ignore, no matter how frequently life rubs it in our faces. In America, the Land of Promise, we awaken each morning clinging to the perception that all the things we enjoy today will be there tomorrow. The truth? Tomorrow makes no guarantees. Ask the people of Kosovo or Russia or Israel. Ask the parents who lost their daughter in a traffic accident.

That's why it's so important to take advantage of every minute you exist. The family that surrounds you today may not be there tomorrow. The job to which you entrust your future and your identity can be gone in a heartbeat. Your health, your bank account, and your home can disappear in an instant. Last night I watched thousands of people from Texas paralyzed by shock as their homes were swept away by unexpected floods. It had never happened before, but it was happening now.

I once did the following exercise with a group of businessmen. I had them write, on five slips of paper, the five most important things in their lives. They folded the slips and held them tightly. Then I informed them a financial catastrophe had destroyed the economy; everyone's wealth was gone. I circled the room with a wastebasket and made them crumple and discard the treasures that were vulnerable to financial collapse.

I repeated this procedure three times, adding factors such as illness, fire, or the death of a loved one into the mix. I was fascinated to see how tightly they clung to some very temporal items. Finally, many of them had only one item left. I insisted that if any catastrophe of any kind could take it from them, they had to relinquish it. What had started out as a lighthearted exercise became a sobering confrontation with matters of who we are and what it is that makes life worth living.

What if Y2K is the disaster some predict it will be? How can I prepare? Sure, I'm taking some physical precautions for Y2K. But the most crucial preparations occur on a spiritual plane. In the end, there are no guarantees for anything on this earth—not even my family. What I must bring myself to understand is that life is about more than this world and its tangible comforts and concerns.

It's about the hope of eternal life. Without that hope, how could there be meaning to anything else? Take a walk in your local cemetery. Its etched stones bear witness to forgotten names—faces that have flickered out in time's expanse. But those engraved, fading epitaphs are not the final word, and therein lies humankind's one substantial hope. Those who have trusted Jesus Christ keep their eyes on the horizon. They look to a world where nothing—let's say the word again: NOTHING—can be taken away.

We must loosen our grip on certain things, and cling ever more tightly to others: friendship with God; our strength in his love. Eternal security enables us to cope with tangible loss. Living in him empowers us to make the most of every earthly minute—and stride fearlessly into uncertainty. Millenniums? They come and go. Why should they trouble the citizens of heaven?

Just a thought:

What is written on the last piece of paper in your hand?

The world and its desires pass away, but the man who does the will of God lives forever. —1 John 2:17

Making a Big "To Do" Out of Life

I backed out of my garage and screeched to a stop in the middle of the road. I was without my daily planner.

Without this book, I was paralyzed; I wouldn't know which end was up. My daily planner runs my world—I only live in it. It's designed to give me more control, and it naturally ends up controlling me.

As I sat fretting over how to go on living without my planner, something important occurred to me. I realized I'd planned the life right out of my life. I was controlling my schedule tightly enough to squeeze out the people I love and the God who loves me.

It all starts with doling out life into those little blank planner spaces. It's human nature for us to fill empty things, including blank planner pages. We fill them with chores to be done, people to contact, phone calls to make, errands to run. Sooner or later we become walking To-Do lists. Things like spontaneous love, refreshing naps, or daydream breaks never find their way into those empty slots. Casual prayer and quiet contemplation go unscheduled—we have To Do. We plan so much life To Do that we don't have time To Do life.

There's another problem: If I plan out every minute, what happens when some emergency, even a small one, arises? I'll tell you what happens: I push all the things on the To-Do list forward. But the blanks up ahead are already full. So I begin to trespass on sacred time. I find myself working during the quiet hours of the evening when I should be relaxing with my family. My wife begs for moments of attention; my children don't even try. God waits, sometimes for days, for a moment alone with the boy he loves. And I keep filling in blanks.

I doubt Adam and Eve had a daily planner. Hmmm. I wonder what it would have looked like if they did.

7:00 A.M. to 8:00 A.M.—Breakfast: honey-covered radishes.
8:00 A.M. to 10:00 A.M.—Name the big animals.
10:00 A.M. to 11:30 A.M.—Name the tiny plants.

11:30 A.M. to 12:00 P.M.—Check on the tree of the knowledge
of good and evil.
12:00 P.M. to 1:00 P.M.—Eat power lunch: fresh fruit.
1:00 P.M. to 3:00 P.M.—Sew fig leaves.
3:00 P.M. to 5:00 P.M.—Look for a good place to hide.
5:00 P.M. to 7:00 P.M.—Boss stops by for a chat.
7:00 P.M. to eternity—Recover from power lunch.

I imagine they had a plan, but they didn't have a planner. Part of the penalty to be paid for the power-lunch debacle was the loss of peace and freedom that existed before. From that moment on there would be pain in childbirth, jealousy, hatred, and daily planners.

Sometimes I wonder if I've become so busy scheduling every moment of my life for success that I miss the one thing I long for most: time to live.

Time to walk hand in hand with my wife—regardless of unfinished tasks.

Time to lie on my back and watch the clouds form and re-form into monsters and angels and things that exist only in the minds of dreamers.

Time to talk to the people I love.

Time to write about the stirrings of my heart.

Time to visit with those people across the street I've never met.

Time to pray—not during scheduled prayer time, but simply because I'm overcome with gratitude, weariness, or joy.

Time to simply talk with God.

Just a thought:

God had a plan, but his plan was about relationships, not achievement. He designed time for being more than for doing. My job requires a hunk of my time for doing. My challenge is to find time in the midst of it all—just for being.

The stuff of real life is not on your To-Do list.

Absolutely Flabulous

When I turned forty, a strange thing happened to my metabolism. It stopped. Now all I have to do is *look* at the fat grams listed on the nutrition label of a candy bar, and they're automatically sucked into me. I know the body is supposed to be a temple, but does it have to be the Mormon Tabernacle? I'd be just as happy resembling a small country church.

How did this happen? I was so skinny in high school that I wasn't safe in a stiff breeze. I didn't want anyone to see me in a bathing suit because of my toothpick arms. I wore a towel around my shoulders until I was safely underwater. Dragging that towel around, no wonder I had trouble swimming.

I tried to gain weight with exercise. I faithfully did my push-ups, my sit-ups, and my throw-ups. I even tried the isometrics theory of muscle development. Isometric exercise consists of tightening every muscle in your body and holding it that way until you change colors.

I even tried isometrics in church. I placed both hands together as if I were praying, then pressed with all my might. My face turned beet-red. I looked up to see the pastor staring directly at me. He wasn't speaking, just looking at me with that "what would Jesus do?" look. My mom and dad were looking at me too. After the service, they did much more than just look at me. They touched me.

Once I passed out while doing isometrics. I took a deep breath and tensed up every muscle in my body; I turned red. Then everything else turned red. Then it all went black. It's true that I didn't gain one ounce of muscle, but those thirty seconds of unconsciousness gave me a nice little break from the tension of trying to gain weight.

I also tried the technique of eating. My mother would pack a school lunch, including an entire loaf of bread with a jar of jelly and one of peanut butter. I'd come home with an empty lunch pail, toothpick arms, and peanut-butter breath that would have offended even an elephant.

When I entered college, the hormones finally kicked in. The exercise I was doing began to pay off. My shoulders suddenly broadened; real muscles began to pop up and stand proudly on my bones.

Unfortunately, the eating began to pay off too. Fresh layers of fat obscured any muscular definition that might lie beneath them. I traded in the loaves of bread for Cinnabuns, summer sausage, and pasta. By the time I reached the age of twenty-five, I tipped the scales at 230—most of it seemingly in my face and thighs. The face is a bad place to carry an extra fifty pounds. My neck disappeared and my cheeks puffed out until it looked as if I were storing nuts for the winter. I couldn't run well because my thighs impeded each other.

I hadn't seen my shoes in over six months. It was time to do something.

My first diet began a roller-coaster ride that runs on into the present day. I tried everything in the book. I drank a popular fluid diet that tasted like chocolate gravel, and I lost fifty-one pounds. But you can't live on that stuff. As soon as I went back to real eating, the weight came back.

I tried the Atkins diet. I restricted myself to meat, fat, and protein and avoided all carbohydrates. The word *carbohydrate* comes from a Latin word meaning "tastes very good." So for six months I ate only high-protein foods with no taste. I lost no weight and drove my cholesterol over the 300 mark. The doctor told me I could market my blood for motor oil.

In the midst of this mess, I decided to have the fat content of my body analyzed by being weighed underwater. I already knew I was too fat—now I was going to pay someone to tell me how much too fat I was. This near-death experience supposedly enables the doctor to determine the exact percentage of fat in your body. You lose a certain amount of weight quickly but painfully. It comes out of your wallet.

The theory goes like this: Muscle and bone sink, fat floats, and money talks. If you give seventy-five dollars to someone with a white coat and a supreme-being air about him, he'll weigh you on dry land, then weigh you underwater. Then he subtracts one figure from the other and determines what percentage of your body is fat. For example, if I weigh 230 on dry land and 30 underwater, then 200 pounds floated.

That means eighty-seven percent of my weight is fat. I am a human bobber. On the other hand, if I weigh 230 pounds on dry land and 200 underwater, then eighty-seven percent of my body weight is muscle and bone. I'm a human anchor, struggling to get off the bottom of the pool.

On the day of my test, the supreme being in the white coat lightened my wallet by seventy-five dollars. That was fifty percent of my net worth. If only he could have eliminated fifty percent of my net weight.

A huge crane extended out over the deep end of a swimming pool. Hanging from the crane was a large swing: the scale. The supreme being's assistant strapped me into the swing, then the white-coated one maneuvered it out over the pool. "Let all the air out of your body," he commanded. I started laughing. As the only male member of my family, I had never been encouraged to let all the air out of my body.

Apparently the great white one had a sense-of-humor content of less than one percent. He gruffly commanded me to breathe out. It was no use reminding him that God didn't intend for us to breathe out before going underwater. He designed us to suck air into our bodies. This is so we can live.

I breathed out until only pitiful little squeaks were coming from my lungs. The swing was suddenly plunged into the water. They can't read the scale accurately until the chair stops bouncing.

Do you know how long it took for the chair to stop bouncing? Let me tell you. In my oxygen-deprived state I thought sure I saw Jesus at the end of a long white tunnel gesturing for me to come to the light. My grandmother was there too, beckoning. I began to move toward the warm glow when I was suddenly jerked from the water. As I gasped for air the light faded, Grandma disappeared, and the white coat proclaimed, "Yep, you're fat!"

"I want a second opinion!" I sputtered, gulping for breath.

"You're ugly too!" he smirked. Just like that I had my diagnosis, I had my second opinion, and I was out seventy-five dollars.

If you still insist on knowing the fat content of your body, I've developed a method that won't cost you a cent. Next time you get out of the shower, grab a stopwatch and stand in front of a full-length mirror totally naked. Start the watch and stamp your foot on the floor as hard as you can. When stuff stops moving, punch the watch and check the time.

I'm down to two days, three hours, and six minutes.

Isn't it funny how much time, money, and emotional energy we desperately invest in the outward appearance of the body? Compare that with the effort put forth to strengthen the inner person, to purify the soul, to build character, and to nurture our relationship with God.

Please don't deluge me with counsel on this matter. In these later years I've gained some measure of success in avoiding the extremes of weight. My secret is simple. I eat healthy foods, I eat decent portions, and I stop eating when I feel full. But now time is taking its toll on my body. My muscles will never be as powerful as they once were. My skin will never be as smooth. There are some things about my outward appearance I will never be able to change.

I'll continue to seek healthy habits for my life, but I refuse to spend an inordinate amount of time trying to do urban renewal on a piece of property I can't hold on to. Jim Elliot put it best: "He is no fool who gives up what he cannot keep to gain what he cannot lose." I cannot keep this body. I have a responsibility to treat it well, but not to obsess over it or worship it.

Mr. Bower, my friend from across the street, was buried yesterday. He and his lovely wife had just celebrated their seventy-fourth wedding anniversary. He was married twenty-four years longer than I've been alive. Mr. Bower was ninety-one years old.

Today, one day after his funeral, it doesn't matter what condition his body was in when he died. It doesn't matter if he was round or thin, or what percentage of his body was fat. The only thing that matters today is the condition of his soul.

I don't know what Mr. Bower looked like when he was young. I do know he was a believing child of God. He glowed with a spirit of love and kindness that hinted of the wonderful faith that sustained him. The body that lay in the coffin gave testimony of a frail old man. But the new Mr. Bower ran to the arms of Jesus with the spirit of a newborn colt.

I didn't hear much of the eulogy. I was thinking about the amount of effort I expend to salvage the appearance of my own aging body compared to the amount of time I spend nurturing the Spirit of Christ within me. I left that funeral determined to seek God's strength to show more kindness, to be more patient, to love more fervently. These are the exercises of character.

Just a thought:

There's not much hope for this body, but eternal possibilities for this soul.

I eagerly expect and hope that I will in no way be ashamed, but will have sufficient courage so that now as always Christ will be exalted in my body, whether by life or by death. For to me, to live is Christ and to die is gain.
—Philippians 1:20–21

Who's in Control?

I couldn't move. I lay strapped to the hospital bed, connected to the world only through a set of tubes. Those lifelines led only to blipping machines and bags of fluid. I couldn't actually see the tubes or the machines, but somehow I knew they were there.

It seemed like muffled shouts and screams were coming from the corridor. I couldn't smell smoke, but I knew there was a fire. The sound of the fire bell swelled and ebbed in rhythm with my level of consciousness. I struggled to wake up and heard a door open. That let in the full fury of the fire bell, and I was startled into a greater state of wakefulness. My chest was pounding like one of those cars with bass speakers that rattle every window in a three-block area.

Suddenly I was fully awake. I wasn't in a hospital at all; I'd fallen asleep in the recliner during prayer. I guess that's why you're supposed to kneel when you pray. That way the pain in your kneecaps keeps you focused so you don't dream about tubes and hospital fires.

The fire bell rang again—it was the phone. My heart rate leaped another ten beats. No matter how hard I try, I cannot coherently answer the phone from a sound sleep. I cleared a few cobwebs from my brain, cleared my throat, and tried to muster at least borderline intelligence. My tongue and my brain behaved as if they weren't acquainted. The planned bright response—"Hello, this is the Davis residence"—came out as "Low, Ooo-izit-n-wachawant."

On the other end of the line was Scott Fowler, the baritone singer for the Cathedrals gospel quartet. We'd shared the platform many times in years past. As of that moment I considered him to be my friend. Yet he seemed unusually nervous as we exchanged small talk for a moment or two. Then suddenly he took a deep breath and blurted out, "Ken, I want to be honest with you and tell you I'm interested in your daughter."

Instantly the lingering cobwebs fell away and my brain and my tongue formed an alliance. I was fully awake and the father in me was on red alert. "Just what kind of interest are you talking about?" I demanded to know.

Scott can sing a high C without breaking a sweat, but now his voice cracked like a mid-pubescent teenager. "Ken, I'm fascinated by your daughter, Taryn, and I'd like your permission to come and visit her."

I was silent. Maybe if I could be quiet for a while, he'd think I'd gone away. Then he would go away. Then the whole thing would go away. Perhaps I could take the family, pack quickly, and find a remote place in the mountains where ... No such luck. He spoke again. "I'd like to get to know your daughter better and explore the possibility of a relationship."

I cut him off. I had no interest in his interest. He was older than Taryn. And he was a musician.

An old musician was after my baby girl! What could be worse? "Thank you, Scott," I said in my best Ward Cleaver voice. "I want you to know you did the right thing by seeking my approval, but under no circumstances will I allow you to do any exploring anywhere in the vicinity of my daughter."

I summoned up all the authority I could muster and put my foot down. That was the way it had to be.

They stepped over my foot and got married that same year. Thanks to the levelheaded intervention of my wife, Diane, and to the impeccable character and determination of Taryn's suitor, I was won over. Taryn was only nineteen when she married. I'm sure you're clicking your tongue and shaking your head in disbelief that I would allow my daughter to marry so young.

Get over it. It happened, and here are six key factors that explain why:

1. Taryn possesses a maturity far beyond her nineteen years.
2. Scott is a man of strong faith in God with a genuine love for Taryn.
3. Taryn does whatever she wants.
4. My wife, Diane, thinks Scott is a gift from God.
5. Ken does whatever Diane wants.
6. Taryn does whatever she wants.

I can read your mind. You're thinking, "Boy, what a wimpy father and weak husband!" You're right! Honesty demands that I admit a couple of truths that apply to both you and me.

First, you and I are both weak. When it comes to the influence we have over the behavior of others, we have much less control than we think we do. In the final analysis, people usually do what they want to do, and not what we want them to do. Parents who struggle with strong-willed or rebellious children will tell you we're only one emphatic "NO!" from discovering this truth. Apart from physical restraint, the compliance of our children, our spouses, and our coworkers to our wishes is pretty much voluntary.

After telling Scott he was not welcome exploring near our home, I hung up the phone. In the other room I could hear Diane clearing her throat with those special little noises that always mean, "I think you've made a mistake."

She needed little encouragement to say what was on her mind. She reminded me that Taryn would soon be leaving our home to live on her own. As difficult as it was for me to accept, the truth was that in a few months she would be making all her own decisions. Diane reminded me that at this critical juncture in Taryn's life, my overprotectiveness might just drive her into the cradle-robber's arms.

She suggested we invite Scott to come to our home, where we could observe the way he treated Taryn. She had a point. This way, I could quickly get my hands on his throat if he acted improperly. The rest is history. We all fell in love with the cradle-robber. Today they're happily married and recently celebrated their first anniversary. Taryn could have searched the rest of her life and not found a more wonderful mate.

But the truth remains: Even if we had not approved of her choice, the final decision would have been hers.

Not all stories have such happy endings. Your child or spouse may well be standing on the edge of a wrong decision. You know it even better than I: All the well-intended advice, all the veiled threats, and all the tearful pleading—all of these still leave the final decision with your loved one. As much as we may feel called to direct the lives of others, in the end we're not holding those keys.

If we are powerless to force others to make wise choices, then where's the hope for wayward loved ones? Where's the hope for continued wisdom in the lives of mature children?

The hope is found in the second truth: God loves your child, your friend, or your spouse even more than you do. Here's the good part: He is in control. As we watch helplessly, God is watching too. But unlike us, he's not helpless. He's at work in their lives with a power far transcending our efforts. The changes may not come as fast as we'd like, as neatly, or in the way we might expect. And the decision to respond to his love is still in their hands. But the fact remains that God's persuasive Spirit can reach into the deep places where all our efforts fail.

Just a thought:

A shift in attitude could make a difference in the life of someone you love. Recognize the limitations of your control. Recognize the unconditional love of God for those you love. Trust him to do his work. This allows you to tone down the barrage of advice and manipulation. It gives you the freedom to simply love them. As you relax and let God do what only he can do, that step of faith is often acknowledged. That alone can make a big difference.

Fathers, [and mothers] do not exasperate your children; instead, bring them up in the training and instruction of the Lord. —Ephesians 6:4

Slow Down and Enjoy the Ride

I was on my way to the airport last Sunday. The woman in the next car was combing her hair and applying lipstick, eyeliner, and mascara—all while maneuvering in and out of traffic. Thank heaven she'd taken her shower before she left home.

I actually saw a man putting in contact lenses as he careened down the freeway at sixty-five miles per hour. One tap on the brakes and those contacts would have been firmly imbedded somewhere near his brain stem. It might have given him the ability to read his own mind, but the pain wouldn't have been worth it.

On still another occasion, I sat at a traffic signal and heard the awful sound of screeching tires. The car skidding to a stop beside me was engulfed in blue smoke and the odor of burning rubber. The driver's face was white as a sheet—except for one brilliant red streak of lipstick zigzagging from the corner of her mouth to the lobe of her left ear. The tube of lipstick was still in her trembling hand. She must have learned her lesson, because she stuck with the clown treatment until she found a safer place to modify it.

I've seen people read books, juggle road maps, and even groom their pets as they rocket down the freeway. Once I watched a man shave and talk on a cellular phone at the same time. He had to have been steering with his knees. I could only hope he was saving his Thigh-Master workout until he got home.

Remember when driving was a full-time job? Whatever happened to both hands on the steering wheel, with one at ten o'clock and one at two? I heard a news reporter say we're more likely to have accidents while talking on cellular phones than while driving drunk. It makes you wonder about drunks who are talking on the phone. Imagine the odds of an accident for wardrobe-changers and makeup-appliers.

Not too long ago, driving was a relaxing pastime. But it did demand that you pay attention. Oh, occasionally you'd see someone singing along with the radio, tapping the steering wheel, head bobbing like one of those back-window pooches. And yes, once in a while you'd see some disgusting (my wife insisted I use that adjective) person driving with their finger in their ear or nose tending to those little personal hygiene items. But you never saw people doing laundry or surfing the Internet. Driving was a welcome respite in a hectic day.

I can remember stressed-out people going for a Sunday drive just to relax. Such a person is considered a road hazard today. Now there's a phenomenon called "road rage." Today, "Sunday driver" is a derogatory reference. You can get shot for taking your time and enjoying the trip. Apparently, the guy shaving and talking on the phone also has a gun in his lap.

Try something for me. On second thought, try it for yourself. Tonight, after the traffic subsides, take a drive. Get away from the city if you can, but this will work even downtown. Leave your guns, razors, and phones at home. Take no makeup. Leave the radio off and look around you as you drive. You'll notice buildings you never knew were there—they built them while you were talking on the phone. You'll see people you didn't know inhabited the planet. And pay very close attention: You may feel the pulse of a city slowing just a little. You might catch a glimpse of the soft quilt of evening beginning to blanket a quiet countryside.

Don't expect some great adventure; just relax and see things. I guarantee you'll feel more alive.

Now transfer that experience to life in general. We've allowed technology to steal too much of the simple beauty of living. We conduct business and tangle with To-Do lists during every waking moment of the day. I know a man who keeps a marker board in his shower so he can work on his To-Do list. While the details of his schedule may be intact, he's missing the personal details that make life rich.

Just a thought:

Before you go to bed tonight, look carefully at the people you love. Consider the world you live in. Make a vow to open the window, slow down, and enjoy the ride.

So do not worry, saying, "What shall we eat?" or "What shall we drink?" or "What shall we wear?" For the pagans run after all these things, and your heavenly Father knows that you need them. But seek first his kingdom and his righteousness, and all these things will be given to you as well.
—Matthew 6:31–33

It's All Downhill from Here

Skiing didn't come easily; I didn't even know skiing language. My first day on the hill I heard someone yell, "Ski, ski!" He was alerting me that a ski was careening down the hill—by itself.

When I first learned to ski, safety straps weren't yet in use. If you lost a ski, it kept racing down the hill at a speed approaching that of a bullet. I've seen a picture of a ski that penetrated a car door. When you hear someone yell, "Ski!" you're supposed to turn and look uphill so you can see what it's going to penetrate.

I didn't know this language. I thought someone was mocking my blundering attempts to make it down the hill. "Ski, ski!" they yelled.

"I am, I am!" I yelled back.

Later that day, I skied to the top of the hill and came down screaming "Toboggan!" People simply skied into the woods to get out of the way. Imagine what *that* would look like embedded in the side of a car door.

Lesson One: If you're going someplace strange, learn the language.

I decided I needed to take a lesson. I was very intimidated by the instructor. "My name is Jacques Benoit [pronounced *Shock Benwah*]," he said in his suave French accent. "Today," he continued, "I ham goeeeng to teesh you how to fall down."

"Excuse me, Mr. Benwah," I interrupted. "I just paid you twenty-five dollars—I'd appreciate it if you would teesh me how to stand up."

I asked for my money back and abandoned the lesson. Dozens of adoring students stayed and learned how to fall gracefully to the ground on command. Later that same day, their skis would cross and they'd all be doing the same clumsy face-plant I was doing. But my fall would seem more graceful, because I was twenty-five dollars richer.

Lesson Two: Never pay money to learn how to fail.

After quitting the lesson I stood in line at the lift with the more experienced skiers. I think I needed more training—I fell while standing in line. My fall triggered a domino reaction. By the time it stopped, there were thirty unhappy people lying on the ground. I didn't want them to know I'd caused the crash, so I just lay there yelling, "Who fell?"

I finally got on the chair lift. Within seconds I was hundreds of feet in the air. I was terrified! I looked over and saw for the first time a man sitting next to me. I have no idea where he came from. Between us was a steel post that connected to the lift cable. It was the only solid thing within reach. I wrapped my entire body around the post. "God loves you and has a wonderful plan for your life," I informed the stranger. "But this is my post. If you touch this post, you will meet Jesus today."

Lesson Three: Take every opportunity to be a blessing.

As I got off the lift, I fell again. I don't know why, but they always ice down the little hill where you get off the lift. I slid to the bottom and desperately tried to stand up. I'd just about made it to my feet when the next person off the lift crashed into me and we both went down.

They don't stop the lift—not for anything. I lay there in the traffic pattern as body after body joined the wiggling pile.

"Who fell?" I screamed as I extracted myself from the group.

Within minutes I was in trouble again. I was standing at the lip of a "black diamond" ski slope—terrified. This slope looked as if it plummeted straight down all the way to a place that does not freeze over. Some of Shock Benwah's practical wisdom came to mind. "If you ever come to a hill that is too difficult for you," he'd said, "then you must traverse!"

Traverse is a French word meaning, "Go across ze hill until you come to ze trees." This allows you to progress more slowly than pointing the skis straight down the hill. "When you get to the othair side of zee slope," Shock instructed, "zen go into a snowplow turn and traverse ze ozzer way."

On this hill, halfway through my first snowplow turn, I was doing eighty miles per hour. I decided there would be no more snowplow turns. I invented my own turn called, "Sit down/turn around." It required twisting my body into positions from which I might never recover. But at least I wasn't moving.

Lesson Four: When in doubt, sit down for a while.

Four hours later I was only fifty feet down the "black diamond" hill. I wouldn't have made it that far if I hadn't been wearing slippery clothes. As I lay there with sweat dripping from every pore in my body, I heard a noise. I looked uphill just in time to see a young boy about twelve years old, swooping down the hill in perfect skiing form. His hair streamed behind him and his cheeks were red from the wind. "Go for it!" he yelled as his body streaked toward me with athletic grace.

I stuck him with my pole. "Go for that, you little shish kebab!"
Lesson Five: If you're old, don't watch young people ski.

But do ski. I've spent years laughing with hundreds of thousands of people over my experiences on the slope. I've met hundreds of those people who identified with the struggles I faced. They've laughed and spoken with animation as they remembered their adventures.

Of course, much of the above is exaggerated. It's tweaked here and there for the sake of fun, but the joy and excitement of trying will never be forgotten. The most energetic and exciting people I know are people who keep exploring the boundaries of life—pushing the envelope. They don't retreat into comfortable patterns, but constantly find new ways to discover the wonders of God in their life.

Just a thought:

Adventure is not just for on-the-edge thrill-seekers. And the Creator of this beautiful world never meant to reserve its enjoyment for the "experts."

Athletically challenged people like me should ski. The tone-deaf should sing. God didn't create couch potatoes. Couches and TVs created couch potatoes. Do something different and challenging today. Get up! Lighten up! Live.

Another Night with the Frogs

The characters and stories of the Bible fascinate me. I've never met anyone who actually read the Bible and persisted in calling it "boring." I'm about to tell you one of my favorite Bible stories. It was written thousands of years ago, yet it describes with perfect precision how we respond to God today. One word in this story jumped out at me. Look at our chapter title, read the story, and see if it doesn't jump out at you too.

But first a little background is in order. Israel's people have been enslaved by the Egyptians. They're being cruelly abused—literally worked to death by their masters. God has chosen Moses to lead his people out of captivity. His job is to petition Pharaoh, the Egyptian ruler, for the Israelites' release. And God gives Moses a powerful negotiating tool: the ability to bring down terrible plagues on the country of Egypt.

In the first plague, every drop of the country's water is contaminated with blood. The stench is unbearable, illness spreads, and clean water is nowhere to be found. Yet the stubborn Pharaoh refuses to let the people go. The Israelites are simply too valuable to him as a cheap source of labor. This brings us to the part of the story that fascinates me. In the midst of an escalating crisis of blood-contaminated water, sickness, and thirst, God commands Moses to bring on another plague:

So Aaron stretched out his hand over the waters of Egypt, and the frogs came up and covered the land. But the magicians did the same things by their secret arts; they also made frogs come up on the land of Egypt. Pharaoh summoned Moses and Aaron and said, "Pray to the Lord to take the frogs away from me and my people, and I will let your people go to offer sacrifices to the Lord." Moses said to Pharaoh, "I leave to you the honor of setting the time for me to pray for you and your officials and your people that you and your houses may be rid of the frogs, except for those that remain in the Nile." "Tomorrow," Pharaoh said. —Exodus 8:6–10

There's the word: *Tomorrow!* What is going through this guy's head? The Bible says frogs are everywhere. Exodus 8:3 spells it out: "They will come up into your palace and your bedroom and onto your bed, into the houses of your officials and on your people, and into your ovens and kneading troughs."

Pharaoh can't even back his chariot out of the garage without killing a hundred frogs. His pizza is covered with frogs. If his home is anything like mine, his wife and oldest daughter have been standing on chairs, screaming ever since the plague began. His youngest daughter has run out of jars in which to collect and accidentally suffocate them. Frogs are everywhere.

Yet, when Moses offers to get rid of them, what is Pharaoh's response? Tomorrow! Does he enjoy frog legs? Is the sound of his shrieking daughters music to his ears? Is he tired of sleeping alone? What could possibly motivate the man to wait until tomorrow if he can resolve the problem today? Why spend another night with the frogs?

This isn't boring reading—this is good stuff! I don't think Pharaoh had any affection for frogs or screaming women. The ruler had an agenda. He had ambitious architectural goals, and they required a labor force. And a labor force required slaves.

If you look carefully, Pharaoh's behavior isn't really so unusual. I've been there myself. I've done that. Cancer ward residents continue to smoke cigarettes through the tracheotomy hole cut into their throats. Why? Because the very habit that is killing them still provides a moment of pleasure. They settle for another night with the frogs. Intelligent people sacrifice reputation, health, and fortune to continue illicit relationships. They do this even when they know they'll be found out. Even after the relationship turns sour; even after they've lost every-thing—they choose to spend another night with the frogs.

I'll never forget the troubled young lady who walked into my office one day. Her dilemma was this: She wanted to live her life in a way that pleased God, but she was confused about what it was that God wanted her to do. Her particular concern was her relationship with her boyfriend. She had been dating this young man for six months. From the beginning of their relationship he had been verbally and physically abusive. Her question to me was: Should she continue to date this man?

Will you be having frogs with that?

I was miserable during the years when I lived a lie. I was one kind of man at home and in church and another kind when no one was watching. Yet I hesitated to turn back to the God who loved me and wanted to take away my guilt and pain. I'd grown comfortable with the frogs.

Sometimes we're just too lazy to call the frog exterminator. It's easier to stay in a rut. We dream of following God's call, but we settle for a life of green-spotted mediocrity because it's more comfortable in the short run. We rationalize one more day of pleasure. We hope that if we ignore the problem, it might go away or spontaneously get better.

These frogs never turn into princes. They multiply and come leaping into every area of life. They demand energy that could be used for good, smelling up lives that were once fragrant with hope and vitality.

Just a thought:

The beauty of knowing a living God is that he's willing to call off the frogs: not tomorrow but today—right now. Don't spend one more minute with the frogs.

So, as the Holy Spirit says: "Today, if you hear his voice, do not harden your hearts. ..." Therefore, since we are surrounded by such a great cloud of witnesses, let us throw off *everything that hinders and the sin that so easily entangles* [frogs], *and let us run with perseverance the race marked out for us.* —Hebrews 3:7–8; 12:1, emphasis added

Burned Bridges and Strawberry Underwear

Sometimes I wonder what our world is coming to. Yes, I'm talking about designer underwear. I'll bet the fig leaves Adam and Eve wore had no little pictures of bears or flags.

It all started when I was a child. It was then popular to have underwear with the day of the week printed on it. This is a concept we men just don't get. As often as I changed underwear as a child, daily underwear was useless. Month of the year . . . maybe. But day of the week?

For my thirtieth birthday, Diane gave me a pair of underwear imprinted with pictures of little strawberries. I laughed—*big* mistake. This was not a gag gift. She found strawberry underwear romantic, and she wanted me to wear it the next time I was away from home to remind me of her. Whatever happened to a snapshot or a greeting card? I'd have preferred to tie a string around my finger.

What if I was in an accident and ended up in the emergency room in strawberry underwear? I agreed to wear it, but I drove more carefully than I ever had before. No one was going to see those strawberries. As I crawled into my hotel-room bed that night, I was tempted to cheat and put on my comfortable old boxers. Then I remembered the look of disappointment on my wife's face when I laughed. The strawberries stayed on.

I don't know how long I slept before a sound at the door startled me awake. I've always felt vulnerable in hotels. I live in fear someone will try to get in while I'm sleeping. I sat up in bed just in time to see a shadow cross the beam of light coming in beneath the door.

Now I was wide awake. Who was outside? Quietly I slipped out of bed and put my eye to the little security peek-hole. I could see no one in the hall. I carefully crouched down and looked under the crack in the door. Nothing.

By this time my heart was pounding. I stealthily unlatched the security chain, unlocked the door, and turned the handle. Without a sound, I eased the door open just a crack and peeked out. Still seeing no one, I opened the door wide enough to stick my head out. Like a very anxious turtle I looked to the left and to the right, but the hall was completely empty. Still, I was a bit confused and frightened as I began to pull the door shut. Then I saw it: Lying on the hall floor was a copy of *USA Today*.

That was all I'd heard: someone dropping a paper in front of each room. With a sigh of relief, I stepped out to get the paper—and heard a terrifying sound.

It was the sound of the door clicking shut behind me. I was now standing in the corridor of a very nice hotel.

Locked out of my room.

Wearing skimpy strawberry underwear.

One of my friends had the same experience on a recent cruise. In the middle of the night, he climbed out of bed to use the bathroom. He pulled the door open, half asleep, and stepped through. The only problem was, he found himself standing not in the bathroom but in the corridor of the ship. My friend was no longer half asleep when he heard his door shut and lock behind him.

Now he faced a dilemma. He had to bang on the door loud enough to wake up his wife, but not loud enough to wake up those in the rooms around him.

When his wife heard him knocking and realized what had happened, she had a dilemma of her own. She could stop laughing and go to the door to rescue him, or she could pretend she didn't know him. It might even be fun to call security and enjoy watching her husband try to explain why he was standing in the hall in his underwear at two o'clock in the morning, knocking on someone's door. She chose to let him in, which probably saved a marriage.

You may be wondering what happened to me. I was traveling alone and had no one to answer my knock. After a moment's panic, I began laughing. I gathered up the *USA Today*, wrapped it around myself, and made my way to the front desk. Mercifully, the halls were empty. I got a new key and left the people at the front desk to entertain themselves at my expense. The way I saw it, I came out ahead—they never saw the strawberries.

You may have already guessed that there are no deeply profound truths to be illustrated here. But there may be a couple of commonsense lessons:

Watch where you're going.

Never shut your doors behind you. And for that matter, don't burn your bridges. As you find new opportunities and face new challenges, it's never a good idea to shut out old friends and important networks. You never know when you'll be knocking on those doors again.

Just a thought:

Be thankful for the little things in life—like *USA Today*!

Who Holds Tomorrow?

The first warning came as I rode back to our rented condo from a beautiful Hawaiian beach. A dull, nagging pain in my shoulder forced me to adjust the seat for a more comfortable ride. We'd saved for years to afford this vacation; muscular pain was the last thing I expected to show up on my itinerary.

Morning: I hadn't slept, and the pain was no longer nagging. It had grown into a full-blown, screaming, eyes-bugging-out kind of pain. It had spread over my back and down my left arm. I could hardly move. I figured I just needed a good day of rest; I sent the rest of the family on its way and tried to get some sleep.

Evening: I was as miserable as I'd ever been. My left arm was on fire. Exhausted from lack of sleep, I tried to make it through one more night. It was Sunday. If I could only make it to morning, I'd go to the doctor the first thing in the morning.

2:00 A.M. By this time I was screaming in pain. I had to crawl on the floor to get to the bathroom, and my left arm wasn't functioning. Up to now I'd blamed it all on a pinched nerve, since I'd had back problems earlier in the year. But this was something much more ominous. Had I waited too long to heed the warning signals?

Diane called 911 and awakened our children. She described my symptoms to the emergency team, and an ambulance was dispatched immediately. I was calm and alert as I waited for the ambulance, but I couldn't move.

Diane almost had her own heart attack from the exertion of trying to dress me. Pajamas would have to do. When the ambulance arrived, three grown men managed to haul my body off the bed, onto a stretcher, and into the van. The balconies of the condo unit were lined with the faces of people awakened by the commotion. "Is he dead?" I heard someone ask.

That was a pretty good question. "Am I dead?" I repeated. "Is this it?"

I knew enough about heart attacks to know I was suffering the classic symptoms. And I'd been a prime coronary candidate for some time. My cholesterol level has been over 300—while anything above 200 is considered dangerous. Even worse, I have only traces of HDL—the "good" cholesterol.

The gawkers filtered back to their rooms as the ambulance began its thirty-mile journey to the nearest hospital. I felt no fear, but there was a sober realization that <u>nothing on this earth is forever.</u> I lay in the back listening to the wailing of the sirens and considering that this might well be one of my last moments. I took comfort in the fact that my entire family, including my daughters and their husbands, were following the ambulance to the hospital. I prayed that God would remain close to me.

The time passed quickly. Soon the ceiling lights in the hospital corridor were racing past my eyes. The next few hours were a blur of blood tests, physical exams, X-rays, and hundreds of questions. Before long the doctor came into the room. "We lack the evidence we need to determine you've had a heart attack," he said. My blood, in fact, was normal and there was no evidence of heart damage. "What do you think it is?" he asked.

"A pinched nerve in my back," I answered with relief. With that, the doctor climbed onto the table with me, secured my permission, and flopped the weight of his body onto mine. It occurred to me there were some strange doctors lurking in Hawaii. I heard a crack—and the pain was instantly gone. I swung my feet over the edge of the bed and stood erect for the first time in days. Nothing remained but a shot to relax my muscles and some pills to calm my nerves. The doctor made me an appointment with a chiropractor, and I was homeward bound.

I got in the car and grabbed the handhold above the window. And that's the last I remember. My family thought I'd died. My hand fell limply to my side, my eyes rolled back in my head, and I began to drool. Then I began to snore.

All those relaxing drugs had hit my bloodstream at the same time. I was out cold. Relieved that I was still okay, my family stopped at McDonald's to eat. They entertained themselves by sticking straws in my nose and placing my body in all sorts of weird positions. I was so dead to the world that I didn't flinch until four hours later.

But what if? I felt no fear that day, but I was confronted with the overwhelming fact that there are no guarantees.

An ambulance came to a house on our street recently. No laughter, no straws, and no jokes had followed that trip to the hospital. One minute a neighbor was there—the next he was gone.

Last week a promising young pastor in my community kissed his new bride as he left to counsel a young couple. He walked through their doorway and was greeted by a volley of gunfire meant for someone else.

What were Christopher Reeves' thoughts just before he was thrown from his horse? I don't know, but I can guarantee they didn't correspond to the magnitude of how his life was about to change.

Life turns on a moment. We don't know what the next one will hold. All that we hold dear can be taken in the next hour. The victims of earthquakes and floods and late-night trips to the emergency room will confirm the truth of this. You and I have our moments of destiny to face. They're unavoidable. We can't predict when they will come or the severity of their impact, but we can be sure that they will come and we can be prepared.

Two facts kept fear from overwhelming me that night. First, I was living with few regrets. I haven't always lived my life with class and integrity. Those who know me best know this about me. God knows it too. But his forgiveness and love left no room for regret. My family had seen the power of God's grace change my life. When my moment came, I knew I was at peace with God and with the people I love.

Second, I realized I'm living with hope. This life is not all there is for me. When I'm done here, I look forward to an eternal life gloriously free of temptation, stress, and pain. One challenge impressed itself upon me as I awoke the next morning. Someone once said to me, "We ought to live every day as though Christ was born yesterday, died today, and is coming again tomorrow."

I want that kind of excitement.

I want that kind of intensity.

I want that kind of hope for my life. And I want it today.

Just a thought:

There's hope for you too. Have you heard the saying, "Here today, gone tomorrow"? That saying really doesn't apply for the man or woman who has trusted in the forgiveness of Jesus Christ. Those who identify with him can say, "Here today, there tomorrow."

Out of Habit

Driving to the airport the other day, I suddenly found myself five miles down the wrong road. I was headed in the opposite direction from where I wanted to go. For twenty years a left turn at this exit took me to the airport. But the highway department had made some changes. A left turn no longer led to the airport; it led to Texas—not a good idea since I live in Colorado.

I missed my plane. I had become a victim of habit. Several days later, my wife was driving me home from the airport when I saw flashing lights ahead. We slowed to a crawl as we passed the same interchange. Someone had lost control because they expected the road to be as it had always been. This time, habit had claimed a life.

There's tremendous power in routine—that's why they call it "force of habit." Habit can hypnotize. It can blind us to the opportunities before us. I fly over one hundred thousand miles a year. Every aspect of travel from packing to check-in to boarding has become part of a routine with me. This isn't necessarily a bad thing. If I had to focus energy on every tiny detail of travel, there would be no room for more productive thoughts. Familiarity allows me to find the airport, buy my ticket, and go to the right gate without giving those actions a lot of thought.

On the other hand, if I allow an ingrained habit to be the only option, the smallest change can cause awful chaos. For example, I'm accustomed to boarding airplanes from the left side. I've done this throughout my long years of travel. All enclosed boarding ramps enter from the left side of the plane. The airline uses the right-side door for loading the galley with the inedible scraps they call food. The Jetway enters the left side. Once on board, I always turn right to be confronted immediately with rows of coach seats, one of which will be mine.

Only once did it happen differently—I entered from the right side. Never before or since have I done that. But this one time I walked down the enclosed boarding ramp fully expecting what I'd faced thousands of times before. I stepped on to the airplane, turned right, and stepped directly into the cockpit.

The effect was overwhelming. This was the shortest airplane in the world: It had only two seats! They were both great window seats, and men in uniform occupied each. I was so disoriented I felt nauseous. Throwing up on the pilots is not a good way to get frequent-flyer miles. I knew something was wrong, yet it took several seconds before I could bring myself to turn around. My seats *had* to be to the right; they were always to the right. I hadn't made a wrong turn. It was the mistake of whomever manufactured the airplane—that's what I stubbornly told myself.

My confusion was quite a source of entertainment for the pilots and flight attendants. And I wasn't the only one who was mystified that day. I sat near the front and entertained myself watching the startled faces of many other passengers. But habit-driven behavior doesn't always bring humorous results. It's painful to discover just how enslaved we can become to doing it the way we've always done it. There are people in our church who sit in the exact same pew in the exact same spot every Sunday. If you were to visit the church and accidentally sit in one of those spots, a cold stare would quickly displace you. These folks are unwitting slaves to habit.

I'm amazed by the habits that control my life—insidious, hard-to-identify kinds of habits:

Patterns of treating my wife and children that have evolved over such a long period of time that I don't even see them as habits.

Patterns of behavior that protect me from pain but also keep me from the richness of intimate relationships.

Patterns of anger that make me an unwitting hostage to a bitter and vengeful spirit.

Patterns of dealing with—or in my case, avoiding—confrontation.

Several years ago my family helped me see how I had used silence and procrastination to avoid confrontation. There isn't a relational version of the "nicotine patch" to help wean me from these habits.

Two factors, God's grace and the simple reality of aging, have had a mellowing effect on my life. I've recognized the destructive habits that had been obscured from my view for years. I've accepted the exciting challenge to change. Creatures of habit are controlled by circumstances. They're too often blind to new opportunity and deaf to the voice of God. It's time to wake up and live.

God specializes in exposing habits and offering the only hope for change.

Search me, O God, and know my heart; test me and know my anxious thoughts. See if there is any offensive way in me, and lead me in the way everlasting. —Psalm 139:23–24

Ordinary People, Extraordinary Wisdom

I continue to gather the best nuggets of wisdom from ordinary people—folks who admit they're simply fellow strugglers in a fallen world. Self-proclaimed experts have little to offer me. They're trapped within the confines of their own expert advice. True wisdom, it seems to me, arises from vulnerability. The experts are closed off from the education failure provides.

No matter who you are, you'll find something in the following list to use today. There's nothing earthshaking here—just the profound stuff of real life and real wisdom, as seen by real people.

Things I've Learned

I've learned I must live so that if someone gossips about me, no one will believe it. (age 39)

I've learned that just when I get my room the way I like it, Mom makes me clean it up. (age 13)

I've learned that children and grandparents are natural allies. (age 46)

I've learned that even when I have pains, I don't have to be one. (age 82)

I've learned that silent company is often more healing than words of advice. (age 24)

I've learned that if you pursue happiness, it will elude you. But if you focus on your family, the needs of others, your work, meeting new people, and doing the very best you can—happiness will find you. (age 65)

I've learned that motel mattresses are better on the side away from the phone. (age 50)

I've learned that regardless of your relationship with your parents, you miss them terribly after they die. (age 53)

I've learned you can't hide a piece of broccoli in a glass of milk. (age 7)

I've learned that the greater a person's sense of guilt, the greater his need to cast blame on others. (age 46)

I've learned that life sometimes gives you a second chance. (age 62)

I've learned it pays to believe in miracles—and to tell the truth, I've seen several. (age 73)

I've learned you shouldn't go through life with a catcher's mitt on both hands. You need to be able to throw something back. (age 64)

I've learned that brushing my child's hair is one of life's great pleasures. (age 29)

I've learned that wherever I go, the world's worst drivers have followed me there. (age 29)

I've learned that singing "Amazing Grace" can lift my spirits for hours. (age 49)

I've learned you can make someone's day by simply sending them a little card. (age 44)

I've learned that if I want to cheer myself up, I should try cheering someone else up. (age 13)

I've learned that when I wave to people in the country, they stop what they're doing and wave back. (age 9)

I've learned that although it's hard to admit it, I'm secretly glad my parents are strict with me. (age 15)

I've learned you can tell a lot about a man by the way he handles these three things: a rainy day, lost luggage, and tangled Christmas tree lights. (age 52)

I've learned that whenever I decide something using kindness, I usually make the right decision. (age 66)

I've learned if you want to do something positive for your children, try improving your marriage. (age 61)

I've learned that making a living is not the same thing as making a life. (age 58)

I've learned that everyone can use a prayer. (age 72)

I've learned I like my teacher because she cries when we sing "Silent Night." (age 7)

I've learned there are people who love you dearly but simply don't know how to show it. (age 41)

I've learned that every day you should reach out and touch someone. People love that human touch: holding hands, a warm hug, or just a friendly pat on the back. (age 85)

My favorite one is written by a ninety-two-year-old man: "I've learned that I still have a lot to learn."

Potential is maximized in the life of any person who never stops learning.

"He's Baaaaaack!"

A woman happened to be looking out the window of her home one day. She was horrified to see her German Shepherd shaking the life out of the neighbor's rabbit. Her family had been quarreling with these neighbors; this was certainly going to make matters worse. She grabbed a broom and ran outside, pummeling the pooch until he dropped a rabbit now covered with dog-spit—and extremely dead.

After a moment's consideration, the woman lifted the rabbit with the end of the broom and brought it into the house. She dumped its lifeless body into the bathtub and turned on the shower. When the water running off the rabbit was clean, she rolled him over and rinsed the other side.

Now she had a plan. She found her hairdryer and blew the rabbit dry. Using an old comb, she groomed the rabbit until he looked pretty good. Then, when the neighbor wasn't looking, she hopped over the fence, snuck across the backyard, and propped him up in his cage. No way *she* was taking the blame for this thing.

About an hour later, she heard screams coming from the neighbor's yard. She ran outside, pretending she didn't know what was going on. "What's happened?" she asked innocently.

Her neighbor came running to the fence. All the blood had drained from her face. "Our rabbit, our rabbit!" she blubbered. "He died two weeks ago, we buried him—*and now he's back!*"

Had the neighbor poked the rabbit or tried to play with him, she would have discovered the truth: The rabbit was dead. And playing with a fluffed-up dead rabbit isn't much fun.

The same is true with fluffed-up dead people. One of the disadvantages of living in an affluent society—meaning most of us—is that it's too easy to get dead and buried *before* we're dead and buried. We clutch our material possessions and social status tightly. We're afraid to take risks, stand out in a crowd, or do anything that could make us look different. In a world of people whose first priority is to maintain the status quo, simply looking alive is too dangerous.

I once spoke with a news anchorman who hated nearly every aspect of his job. When I asked him why he didn't quit, he said he'd come too far to turn back now. To search for something more significant in life would mean taking a pay cut and relinquishing a few job perks. So every day he gets up and heads for a job he hates, so he won't lose what he's gained. And just what has he gained? It sounds like a fluffed-up dead rabbit to me. All over America people remain in jobs they hate so they can buy stuff they don't need to impress people who don't care.

God created you for so much more than that. Could it be time for you to take a deep breath and really live again?

Take some risks. God's plan for your life was never about being propped up in a cage. I've met dozens of people who finally trusted God and made their escapes. Some changed jobs; some changed attitudes; some took the initiative and summoned up the courage to live out their convictions.

There are some who are living with fewer financial resources than before, but they're experiencing an excitement and a renewed faith they never knew was possible. The renewed fire in their lives leaves no doubt they're alive.

Just a thought:

Jesus is about life. If you feel as if you've been shaken, hosed off, and propped up to dry, chances are it's time to take a look around. God wants you to live. People will be delighted and amazed that you're back.

He is no fool who gives up what he cannot keep to gain what he cannot lose.
                                                            —*Jim Elliot*

I'll Sing for You, Daddy

The program was set to begin. I settled back in my seat, surrounded by a sea of eleven thousand faces. At the conclusion of a thirty-day tour I was physically exhausted and emotionally spent. Most of all, I was adjusting to the news of my youngest daughter's engagement.

I was feeling sorry for myself—old and deserted, an aging model-T putt-putting along in a world exceeding the speed limit. The people seated around me in the arena were pausing from their hectic lives to sing and pray and laugh and learn together. From my vantage point, it was just another stress-filled speaking engagement. Beside me was Taryn, the lovely daughter who'd betrayed me by getting engaged so young. I waited with a burdened heart for the beginning of the festivities.

The lights began to dim. Suddenly the room was filled with wonderful music: the soaring brass of an orchestra, the harmonies of several college choirs joining their voices in song. They sang "Behold the Lamb of God" as a stately procession of young people bore colorful banners, each displaying a name for our awesome God.

I was deeply moved. Then again, in my physical and emotional state I would have been deeply moved by a piano-recital rendition of "Chopsticks." Still, all the pageantry before me caused tears to stream down my face.

Then Walter Wangerin, one of the finest storytellers I know, stepped to the platform. He stood and faced the choir silently for a moment. Finally he spoke: "Behold the Lamb of God!"

He paused as he looked over the youthful faces of the choir. "Will you sing like that tomorrow?" he asked. "When I'm very old; when I've lost my hair and my sight; when I've lost my self-control so that I cry more often than I would wish, and I've lost my bodily control so that I befoul myself—when I'm no longer pretty and I know that I'm no longer pretty, will you come and sing to me then?"

Wangerin's message was based on Exodus 20:12—"Honor your father and your mother, so that you may live long in the land the LORD your God is giving you." His challenge was to reflect the love of the Lamb of God by loving and honoring our aging parents. That message touched the raw edges of my soul. Eleven thousand people sat in silence as he closed his message with a powerful illustration. The only sound that accompanied his voice was the hushed weeping throughout the building.

He told of visiting his friend Mel on a crisp autumn afternoon in Wisconsin. Mel spent much of his time reading and studying in his parlor, where he could be with his aging mother. As Walter entered his friend's home, he was enveloped in the wonderful aroma of apple pie. "Oh, I see your mother is baking pies," Walter said with a smile.

"No," Mel answered. "I see to the necessary things now." Looking around, Walter understood what he meant. There was a pool of light cast by Mel's reading lamp, and just beyond it, in a bed, was Mel's ailing mother. Walter had known her for years. Now she sat propped up, her face an empty slate. Mel made introductions as though they'd never met. As Walter reached forward and shook her hand, her watery blue eyes never gazed higher than his stomach. Walter sadly comprehended: A dear old friend no longer knew him.

After sharing a walk and a slice of apple pie with his friend, Walter retired to bed. In the middle of the night he was awakened by a sound from the parlor. Someone seemed to be in great pain. There were awful, inarticulate screams coming from downstairs: "Yeeeahhhh! Naaaaah!" He rose quickly, wrapped a robe around himself, and hurried down to the parlor.

Mel wasn't in his chair. With eyes adjusting to the darkness, Walter could see his friend Mel kneeling beside the bed of his mother. He motioned for Walter to be seated. As Walter did so, he became aware of an awful odor, and he knew what his dear friend was doing—he was changing his mother's diapers. He was cleansing his mother with tenderness and grace. He was honoring her in the very spirit God prescribed for the honoring of parents.

And as he did so, he softly sang. He was singing lullabies to her in the language she knew as a child. "And you know what she was doing?" Walter asked eleven thousand listeners on the edges of their seats. "In a lusty voice, she was singing along: 'Yeeeahhhh . . . Naaaaah . . .'"

Walter testified, "As she sang along with her son, I know she was young and beautiful once more. She was in no prison and under no slavery, neither of sin nor of body. Mel's mother stood before the congregation with bows in her hair. She was once again in her homeland, where all was new and all was good. And she was singing at the top of her lungs to her Father in heaven."

There wasn't a dry eye in the audience. My shoulders heaved as that deep part of my soul longed to be honored and loved with such tenderness. At that moment, Walter Wangerin turned once again to the choir. "And when I come to die, O my children—will you remember me?" he asked. "When I have no hair or teeth or continence or sense left; when I have no beauty and know that I have none; when mostly I smell and I shudder and I cannot control my tears, will you come to me? With tenderness and conviction and strength, will you sing the songs that your parents knew in their childhood? So that they may be honorable again; so that this land will last; will you sing to me then?"

I buried my head in my hands and wept openly as Walter softly, tenderly, led the audience in the first verse of "Jesus Loves Me." I felt an arm ease around my shoulders. Gently a hand pulled my head close, and the voice of my beautiful eighteen-year-old daughter whispered in my ear:

"I'll sing for you, Daddy. I'll sing for you."

All the stress and tension melted away. Even as I wept, I basked in the kind of love that every heart craves—the kind of love that changes the world. Behold the Lamb of God!

Just a thought:

Sing for someone today.

The Author of Joy

There was a subtle message hidden just beneath the surface of the legalistic theology I knew as a child: *If it's fun, it must not be Christian.* The excitement and laughter generated by a swim party or a pizza feast were not sanctified until they were legitimized by a serious devotional. To skip this step of blessing placed the aforementioned activities squarely in the category of sin.

My childhood picture of God was that of a stern and watchful policeman whose eyes scanned the earth for any signs of merriment. At the sound of laughter, his cosmic sandal would come smashing down on the offenders as a thunderous voice cried, "NO."

Since then I've come to believe that God is the author of joy, the fountain from which pure laughter springs.

The world is desperate for any sign of joy. Men and women have searched the realms of materialism, hedonism, and even religion looking for joy. They've even peeked into our churches. They've studied the faces of those who claim to know the author of joy—and found nothing joyful at all. Churches ought to be filled not only with the sound of solemn prayers and practical lessons from God's Word; laughter, too, should be heard bouncing from our walls.

One Sunday as we prepared for church, Diane got what I call a wild hare. A wild hare is a small rabbit that has never been domesticated. Whenever you get a wild hare in a tight spot, it kicks and jumps around for no apparent reason. Occasionally it may even try to bite someone. If you get several wild hares over a short period of time, then it's said that you had a bad hare day.

Diane called the family together and began to rage about kids moving around in church. "I'm sick and tired of seeing teenagers treat church like a rock concert," she ranted. "During the sermon they get up in herds to go to the bathroom, and I'm sick of it."

Evidently she'd been stewing about this for a long time, because this was the wildest hare I'd ever seen. She'd actually given it enough thought to work out a solution. Establishing eye contact, she announced the edict: "This family is not going to be a part of this travesty," she seethed, her face turning a unique shade of red. "I'm making a new rule. Whatever you have to do, you do it before you get to church. Once we're in church, you will sit down and you will not move."

She spat the last three words out one at a time with great emphasis. "Do . . . you . . . understand?" she demanded, staring wild-eyed, waiting for an answer.

"Yes ma'am," I said. Then she turned to the children and repeated the rule for them.

When we got to church, we were ushered to a seat near the front. I began to squirm. We stood a few minutes later to sing a hymn, and I became acutely aware that I was going to have to break the rule. Of all Sundays for nature to call, it had to be the Sunday of the wild hare. As the congregation sang, I leaned over and whispered to Diane, "I have to go."

She turned quickly and whispered with great hostility, "You will not move. You know the rule."

"I know the rule, and it's a good rule," I said, "but I have to go." "If you leave," she hissed between clenched teeth, "you're going to set a bad example."

I was doing that little have-to-go dance now. "If I stay, I'm going to set a bad example," I blurted out and exited to the back, trying to walk with some semblance of normalcy. I took care of business and came back quickly. I had no desire to cause any more trouble.

I made it back before the hymn was completed. I quickly slipped into the pew and sat down. I didn't even have to look to know Diane was furious. I could feel hostility and anger radiating from her body. In an effort of reconciliation, I put my arm around her and gave a little hug. I was shocked to feel her pushing me away, digging her elbow into my ribs. Here we were on God's day in God's house, and my wife was elbowing me because I did what had to be done.

I turned to tell her to quit being so angry, only to discover she wasn't my wife. I'd absentmindedly slid into the wrong pew. I was hugging a woman I'd never met while my wife sat directly behind us, watching the whole thing. I'm pretty certain that's where the hostility was radiating from.

The pastor saw the whole thing play out. He tried his best to continue, but he lost the battle and burst into laughter; then the congregation lost it. When the laughter subsided, the pastor wiped the tears from his eyes and proclaimed, "Brothers and sisters, if God can save that man, then God can surely save you."

As I left the church after the service, a very angry woman approached me. "What do you think God thought of that?" she spat. Then she turned on her heel and stomped away.

She might as well have stabbed me with a knife. My blunder was an honest mistake. I would never intentionally do anything to call attention to myself during worship, or to destroy the sanctity of a church service. The picture of the unsmiling police-state God came into focus again for the first time in years.

I was sulking during the drive home, and Diane asked me what was wrong. I somberly repeated the woman's angry words. Diane started laughing. "What *do* you think God thought?" she asked me.

Had God watched from heaven, filled with rage? I think not. Perhaps he saw and called out, "Angels, hurry! Looketh at this idiot! I love that man; I gave him a twisted mind, and look—he's using it!"

God's justice is real. It's not aimed at some mistake made by a half-witted comedian. It's the fairness of his justice and the wonder of his grace that make joy possible. Real joy comes from knowing God forgives you, from knowing that the Creator of the universe loves you and cares about your life. Those are sources of joy that remain firmly in place even in the times when laughter is impossible. I've seen that joy at funerals, its strong foundation bringing hope to what would otherwise be a hopeless day.

Just a thought:

Joy and laughter are two different things. But when your feet are firmly planted on the joy that comes from knowing God's love and forgiveness, laughter is an inescapable by-product.

Trust him, and he will lighten your load. Know him, and you will know real joy. Then you can throw back your head and laugh as you've never laughed before.

A Shelter in the Time of Storm

Jamie and Bill had saved for several years and traveled six hundred miles. Now they were setting out to fulfill the dream of a lifetime.

They had chosen Mount Columbia because it was a relatively simple climb. After a full day of hiking, they set up a base camp near the timberline and planned their assault of the summit the next day. This would be their first ascent of a "fourteener"—a mountain fourteen thousand feet high. It was almost their last.

The couple slept late the next morning and found they were still tired when they woke up; their bodies were adjusting to the high altitude. After a quick meal they began the day's climb.

Several hours later the couple stood at the summit. They surveyed a spectacular panorama spread before them—nature's raw splendor at its finest. To the north they could see Mount Harvard and Mount Elbert. Eastward, Buffalo Mountain stood guarding a view stretching almost to Denver. Toward the west, jagged sunlit peaks braced an ominously black sky that signaled an approaching storm. Jamie and Bill decided to start their descent early. They were eager to make it back to camp before the storm hit.

The two climbers were only halfway to timberline when they were overtaken by a menacing blackness that stretched across the sky above them. Bill looked back to tell Jamie to hurry. He was horrified by what he saw—every strand of her shoulder-length blonde hair was standing straight up in the air. Bill could feel the hair rising on his own neck. The air was charged with electricity.

When he removed his hat, his hair flew upward. Even the hair on his arms was standing straight out. They might have kidded each other about looking like walking cartoons, but the danger wasn't amusing; it was palpable. Bill and Jamie knew they were the highest points on a barren slope. Their bodies were creating a perfect pathway for a discharge of millions of volts of electricity. They had become human lightning rods. Bill shouted to Jamie to run for a jumble of monstrous rocks a hundred yards down the slope. The bottom dropped out and the rain began to fall just as they reached the outcropping. They dived into a crevice between two great boulders, as a roar and a blinding flash of light pinned them to the ground.

Bill says the next twenty minutes were the most terrifying of his life. In a matter of seconds, the rain soaked them to the bone. Lightning was striking so close that it merged with the thunder into a series of deafening, blinding discharges that assaulted them without warning. The massive boulders around them trembled at the high-voltage blasts. And the whole world smelled of ozone.

Eventually the storm resumed its eastward journey. It left behind an innocent blue sky, and the warm air returned. Bill and Jamie admired the placid canopy and offered a heartfelt prayer of gratitude. Arriving safely back at camp, they had a new respect for the power and deadly speed of storms.

I've learned to share that respect. Diane and I took my daughter Taryn and her husband Scott on a camping trip recently. I was napping in the tent as the rest of the family sat under a clear sky playing a card game. We had pitched our tent at about ten thousand feet. The temperature was eighty degrees and just to the west was a darkening sky.

This storm hit without warning. An earsplitting clap of thunder sent the cards spiraling through the air. I exploded from the tent, half-asleep. With the boom of thunder, hail began pounding the earth, driving all of us into the shelter of our tents. The temperature dropped almost forty degrees; the sky turned an ugly greenish-black.

Lightning crashed continuously as four inches of hail covered the ground. Then the rain began. As torrents of water fell I called out to see if everyone in the other tent was okay. Everyone beside me had taken shelter in the only other tent. I rolled over to hear their reply over the roar of the thunder. As I did, I placed my hand on the floor of the tent; it was like a waterbed. Our tents were floating in three inches of ice-cold water.

Of course we survived, or I wouldn't be writing this. That day I, too, gained a new respect for the power and danger of a storm. Without the proper shelter and dry clothing, we'd have been in serious trouble. A friend sent an e-mail message asking how we fared in the violent weather. My answer to him will give you a capsule of our escape from the mountain.

Wednesday: 2:00 p.m.—Eighty degrees; ten thousand feet; sunshine.

Wednesday: 2:10 P.M.—Forty degrees; four inches of hail; three inches of water in the tents. Everything soaked and muddy; two hours of hail, lightning, and torrential rain.

Wednesday: 4:00 P.M.—Women vote to leave mountain NOW!

Wednesday: 4:01 P.M.—Men racing down the mountain to get four-wheel-drive vehicle and comply with women's request.

Wednesday: 6:30 P.M.—Everyone watching TV in a mountain cabin. Everyone dry. Women happy. Men happy.

It was easy to make light of the event now that we sat warm, toasty, and dry in our cabin. But at the height of the violence, we felt fear and an incredible sense of helplessness. As I sat in church not long ago, we sang a song about a different kind of storm, the kind that wreaks havoc in our daily lives. I remember thinking that I had never really had a storm in my life. There had been brief periods of darkness, occasional lightning bolts, but never the kind of destructive power I'd seen in other lives. Then I read a passage from Ephesians 6:

For our struggle is not against flesh and blood, but against the rulers, against the authorities, against the powers of this dark world and against the spiritual forces of evil in the heavenly realms. Therefore put on the full armor of God, so that when the day of evil comes, you may be able to stand your ground, and after you have done everything, to stand. Stand firm then, with the belt of truth buckled around your waist, with the breastplate of righteousness in place, and with your feet fitted with the readiness that comes from the gospel of peace. In addition to all this, take up the shield of faith, with which you can extinguish all the flaming arrows of the evil one. Take the helmet of salvation and the sword of the Spirit, which is the word of God. And pray in the Spirit on all occasions with all kinds of prayers and requests. With this in mind, be alert and always keep on praying for all the saints. —Ephesians 6:12–18*

We're usually oblivious to the spiritual battle around us. We may not hear thunder or see lightning, but nevertheless the storm rages. We're constantly in the vortex of a deadly storm. The struggle is a spiritual one and the objective of the deceiver is nothing less than our total destruction. The storm I experienced on the mountain started in clear skies. Even in the brightest sunshine we should constantly walk with full armor and in the shadow of God's protection.

Just a thought:

Don't get caught without the armor. Never cease thanking God for the protection he provides from the storms you never see.

Empty Nest

. . . It's for the birds!

On August 21, 1997, the Davis nest emptied and the big birds got confused. The patter of little feet, the all-night video parties and the one-hour showers ceased. We may never again hear the howl of "I'm hungry."

Our children have flown the coop. I learned about the empty nest in grade school. The story went something like this: First the mother bird lays the eggs; then the dedicated mother and father bird patiently sit on the eggs for several weeks to keep them safe and warm.

Stop right there! What's so dedicated about that? Birds are wimps—Diane and I sat on these eggs for *twenty-two years!*

I was sitting on eggs the day we rushed Traci to the hospital after she spilled boiling water on her legs. We sat on eggs at night when they were babies, lying awake listening for the sounds of breathing. Diane sat on eggs for hours in the school parking lot waiting to pick the nestlings up after school. I sat up waiting for them to come home from dates. We sat at dance lessons, tennis lessons, music lessons, and driving lessons. Don't give me this stuff about dedicated birds; I have permanent egg prints in my backside!

In the cushy bird world, the parents search for worms to feed hungry, gaping mouths. No worms for *my* chicks. They demanded Nike tennis shoes, a prom dress, a cheerleading outfit, dance clothes, designer jeans, perfume, and transportation. And what bird ever paid for a wedding? I would have gladly hunted down a few grubs. It's one thing to regurgitate a couple of insects to feed a hungry mouth, but no bird ever had to regurgitate the entire contents of a wallet every day for twenty-two years.

For birds, the empty-nest thing is final. A gentle nudge out of the nest and the little bird struggles to take flight, never to be seen again . . .

Yeah, right! Our birds want the best of both worlds. They're ready to fly after the fifth grade. They dive from the nest in a convulsive flurry of independence, then circle the tree with beaks open for the next fifteen years.

I'm not complaining. I'm just saying the "dedicated bird" thing is *way* overrated.

In the bird world, the little ones are pushed out of the nest. Then the parents simply turn their backs and make some more eggs. Diane and I don't fit the bird mold very well. We cannot bear to turn our backs—and we're certainly not going to lay any more eggs!

Now I sit anxiously at the edge of the nest, waving worms (actually, my wallet), hoping they'll come back. I don't want them to stay. I don't want to sit on them again. I just want to talk, to laugh, to see them fly. You know, big bird stuff: "How's your new nest coming? Any eggs on the way? Have you heard about the Finch family?"

After a day or two, they can fly away without having to be dropkicked. We'll be glad to be alone again and sad to be alone again. I hope they won't fly too far.

Nope, empty nests are for the birds. Our nest is empty, and the big birds are lonely and confused. Our lives used to revolve around our children. Now the baby birds are gone; we only have each other . . .

Come to think of it, maybe this empty-nest thing has some possibilities.

Just a thought:

Maybe empty-nest time is a good time to become lovebirds once again.

Say What You Mean and Mean What You Say

The older I get, the more I find myself saying, "I wish I could do that over again." I don't have a closet full of regrets—it's more like a shoebox. Still I'd like a chance to do some things differently.

For one thing, I'd love another shot at raising my kids to love and honor God. Too often I avoided overt expressions of faith in my daily life. I was acting out my feelings toward those who cheapened faith language—people such as the young man I met more than thirty years ago. He came to my door and introduced himself. "I'm Ken Davis," I responded. "I'm glad to meet you."

To which he responded, "Praise the Lord."

"Please sit down," I said.

To which he responded, "Praise the Lord."

After a few minutes, I excused myself to go to the bathroom. "Praise the Lord," he said. Uncomfortable with this encounter, I remained in the bathroom as long as possible. Conversation was basically limited to three words on his part, and the vibrant phrase had lost much of its meaning in its endless repetition.

I returned from the bathroom just in time to see a snowplow passing the window. This was Minnesota, where snowplows cruise by at forty miles per hour and scatter snow twenty or thirty feet. But this one had picked up some rocks, which shattered all the windows in the left side of the young man's van. "That snowplow just broke all the windows in your van!" I shouted.

The young man ran to the window and spat out a "Praise the Lord"—through clenched teeth.

I couldn't take it any longer. "Yes, isn't that a @#*&$*&!" I can assure you it was a very mild curse, but the young man stared at me as if I'd just sacrificed a virgin on a pagan altar.

I simply couldn't tolerate insincere God-talk. "Ever since you came in here," I said to him, "you've been taking lovely words and cheapening them. When the snowplow broke your windows you used 'Praise the Lord' as an expletive."

The Third Commandment ("You shall not misuse the name of the LORD your God") may well be the most misunderstood. My own oath on that occasion wasn't the target of this commandment; it was the thoughtless, insincere use of God's name.

My response should have been more loving and gentle, but I've always had an aversion to casual Christianese. Some folks use that terminology sincerely and meaningfully. For others it's simply pious slang—the language of a subculture. And incidentally, it's a language found exclusive and confusing by those who don't know Jesus Christ.

I once complimented a young lady who sang in our church. I stopped her in the foyer and said, "Thanks for your song today. The words really touched me."

"It wasn't me singing," she oozed, "it was God."

I wanted to respond, "God can sing a lot better than that!"

Wouldn't a simple "thank you" have sufficed? Even a sincere "praise the Lord" would have seemed more appropriate. I know I've tended to react a bit too harshly. I'm certain there were many genuine believers whom I wrongly branded as insincere. But I felt most of these folks were speaking God-talk not out of their hearts, but because they felt it was expected of them.

I grew up sharing meals at church members' homes. Insisting we give thanks, the host would pray, "Lord, bless our conversation around this table, and bless this food to the use of our bodies. Amen." Then, in the next breath, he'd verbally assassinate the pastor or some other church member. This made the blessing seem as spiritually questionable as the family "devotions" I sat through. In those meetings, the real agenda was making us face the music for the things we'd done wrong the previous week.

Those things remain in a little mind for a long while—and I have a little mind.

Unfortunately my reaction overcompensated for the problem. I hurried to the other extreme. I was comfortable expressing my faith from a platform but reluctant to do so in more intimate settings. I was sincerely afraid of trivializing things I valued deeply.

Many meals in our home went unblessed with prayer. I made several attempts to start family devotions, but they never lasted long. I rarely said the beautiful words "Praise the Lord" in front of my family. I failed to glorify God verbally in everyday life. Oh, how I wish I could do it over. My children inherited my suspicion of time-honored expressions of praise.

I grew up without the joys of hearing Sunday's phrases and praises on a daily basis; so did my children. I never truly realized this until a couple of years ago. I'd been invited to join songwriters Bill and Gloria Gaither for a special service in Alexandria, Louisiana. We were guests of the Pentecostals of Alexandria. These were people who praised the Lord without shame in their church services and their personal lives. I'm not a Pentecostal, yet I was never uncomfortable in their presence. The choir in this church is one of the best in the nation. If their music doesn't stir your soul, nothing will.

That night there were great musical anthems, wonderful testimonies, and outstanding gospel music from the Gaither Vocal Band. I was scheduled to speak. The church's pastor was moderating the program, and his young son interrupted him by walking up onto the platform. The pastor stopped speaking, stepped away from the podium, and grabbed his son by the head. I thought, "Oh no, he's going to break the boy's neck in front of the entire congregation."

Instead, he pulled the boy's head close and whispered something in his ear. Then, in front of everyone, he kissed his son. He stood and watched as the boy unself-consciously walked across the stage and out a side door.

What was this? Could it be a Pentecostal ritual I didn't know about? The pastor joined me again on the front pew. As we stood to sing I asked, "What was that all about?"

"Oh," he said in a matter-of-fact tone, "it's past my son's bedtime. Every night before he goes to bed, I pray with him. I thank God for giving me my son, and I pray he'll send angels to protect him. Then I tell my boy how much I love him, and I kiss him. Even when I'm on the road," he continued, "I often excuse myself from a service or meeting, step into the hall, and call my son to say 'I love you.' I've only missed a handful of nights in his entire life."

Spontaneously I began to cry. "Where did you learn to do this?" I asked.

"My dad did it for me every day of my life," he replied.

"Will you be my dad for awhile?" I blubbered.

How my heart ached for those consistent expressions of faith and love in the early years of my life. How I wished I'd given my own children such a legacy.

But God is setting my spirit free. Not long ago I was walking in the mountains when I came over a ridge and was treated to a majestic view.

Low clouds filled the valleys; a promising morning sun lit the jagged peaks with a soft glow. Instinctively I fell to my knees. "My God is an awesome God," I whispered over and over. The tears began to flow and the whisper turned to the song written by the late Rich Mullins:

My God is an awesome God.
He reigns from heaven above,
With wisdom, power, and love.
My God is an awesome God.

I still refuse to speak Christianese just because other people speak it. But I'm not afraid to have someone see me kneeling on a mountainside frightening God's creatures with my praise.

When I feel that the Lord needs to be praised, I'm going to praise him. The other day I addressed a group of educators. At the conclusion of my presentation, I received a standing ovation. As the applause subsided, I stepped back to the microphone and told them what I'm telling you. I encouraged them to never be afraid of leaving a verbal legacy of godly gratitude. "Although the law may prevent you from leaving such a legacy in the classroom," I challenged them, "the law cannot prevent you from using those expressions in your personal life."

I told them how sorry I was that I hadn't left my children such a legacy.

Just a thought:

See, I'm learning. I still have a long way to go. The old suspicious nature dies hard. But God has brought me a long way. And he will lead me home.

Praise the Lord!

Rest in Peace

I'm too exhausted to stay up another moment, yet I'm unable to rest.

For me, that's a formula for sheer misery. I lie alone in some hotel, knowing I must rise at five o'clock in the morning to catch a plane; but sleep will not come. My feet keep jumping and scaring me to death. It's embarrassing to admit my own feet can frighten me.

No position is comfortable for more than thirty seconds on such nights. I fold my pillow into a hundred different configurations, but each one feels like a chain-link fence. I develop the hearing of Superman, picking up faucets dripping four rooms away. A fly trapped in the window sounds like a chain saw bouncing in a barrel. Every passing car, every flushing toilet, every guest stepping from the elevator—every new sound becomes my own personal alarm clock, snatching sleep from the jaws of exhaustion.

I gradually begin to doze off. I reach semiconsciousness. I'm rounding third base . . . and a piece of lint falls to the floor, jarring me wide-awake. I look at the alarm clock: It's midnight. If I get to sleep now, I tell myself, at least I'll get five hours of sleep. Two minutes later, I look at the clock and it's 1:30 in the morning.

I'm drifting off again at two. "Clank," says the air conditioner. The unit kicks in. All hotel A/C fan blades are warped. They clank and scrape in ever-increasing tempo. Finally they reach screeching crescendos of torture that guarantee hours of full consciousness.

The air conditioner stops squealing at fifteen minutes after two o'clock. If I go to sleep now, I'll have a little over two hours. I can make it on two hours just this once. The last thing I remember is the red glow of the clock showing a quarter to four. Deep sleep arrives—an hour and fifteen minutes of it—then an alarm jerks me from paradise into a sluggish stupor that will last all day. It's a feeling of profound weariness that makes me feel sick to my stomach.

But there are other kinds of weariness just as debilitating. We live in a tired world, filled with people desperately churning to keep up with life's demands; their spirits, if not their bodies, are close to collapsing. It's worse than missing sleep. Our most successful leaders often crave a season of rest, but it's unattainable to them.

Vacations are like fluffing the pillow. We fluff the pillow with a vacation, hoping for the refreshment we yearn for from the depths of our souls. We fluff the pillow with greater responsibility and higher-level jobs, believing we can buy a little rest with the salary increase. But true rest isn't for sale.

I decided to bring this issue to the circle of friends in my small group. I asked them to pray about the pressures I was feeling. None of these demands had been forced on me; each one was an opportunity I'd pursued freely and tenaciously. They were symbols of success, opportunities many people dream of having. One of those was the chance to write this book.

That night I asked for prayer and strength. One of my friends in the group put his hand on my shoulder and asked, "Ken, when do you rest?"

The tears came suddenly and unexpectedly. I couldn't hold them back. The simple word *rest* triggered within me a desire far more essential than success or recognition or material gain. It was the desire to close the eyes of my soul and find refreshment and peace—a time without anxiety that would revive and strengthen me for what lay ahead. My life was an unbroken string of alarms and noisy air conditioners and buzzing flies. The weariness of my soul had begun to wear on my body. I'd lay awake at night worrying about how to satisfy all the demands, only to wake up the next morning too tired to function.

I know I'm not alone in this struggle. Several years ago I spent three days with two of my friends. We prayed together, played golf, told big lies about our accomplishments, and discussed how we could be better fathers, husbands, and followers of Jesus.

On the last day, as we sat on the back porch watching the sunset, one of my friends asked a question that galvanized the group: "What do you most look forward to in heaven?" The air was thick with silence. Each of us was suddenly in deep emotional water. The vice president of development for a major national ministry, an associate pastor of a growing church, and a humorist with a twisted mind were suddenly bonded by a resonating question.

My friend Mel said it for all of us. He wistfully described his hopes for eternity. It wasn't about streets of gold or reunions with loved ones;

it was about rest. "I dream of running to Jesus," he said. "I dream of having him gather me in his arms, hold me tight, and say, 'It's okay now. You're safe. Now you can rest.'"

After blubbering like idiots for a while, we decided together that some of that hope of rest was available now. After all, to a group of encumbered people in his day—and to us frazzled people in this day— Jesus said:

> *Come to me, all you who are weary and burdened, and I will give you rest. Take my yoke upon you and learn from me, for I am gentle and humble in heart, and you will find rest for your souls. For my yoke is easy and my burden is light.* —Matthew 11:28–30

Jesus isn't suggesting that life will be easy. The point is that if we trust him to provide direction for life, the burden will become bearable. It's the carrying of that burden ourselves that crushes us. Without his power, even the smallest task is exhausting. It's my tendency to take the burden of the world on my own shoulders. I depend on my talents, my health, and my ability to get things done—all the while knowing I'm incapable of ensuring even the simplest of outcomes.

To be everything for everybody seems very spiritual, but it's precisely the opposite of spiritual. I must remind myself again and again that rest is only available in Jesus. He wants us to take upon ourselves only what he asks, and then to simply trust him for the power to prevail. My health, my gifts, and my most basic ability to function are all in his hands. If an accident or even death changes the course of my life, I'm still in his hands.

By taking his yoke and trusting him, I've begun to know a measure of rest I never knew before. What a relief to depend on him. My effectiveness as a communicator, the future of my work, and even the completion of this book is in his hands. And as my soul finds refreshment, my body benefits from untroubled sleep.

I find guilt-free moments to rejoice in his creation. I spend time with him in prayer. I know it won't be a once-and-for-all solution. Sooner or later I'll heft all the responsibility back to my own shoulders. Then I'll once again hear his gentle voice: "Come, my weary friend, and trust me. I won't ask any more of you than you can handle. Let me bring you the rest your soul desires."

In a treadmill world, God offers moments of respite and peace for your soul. Even though the road may be difficult, in this very moment take comfort from his tender promise of rest. One day you'll be able to bury your face in his breast and hear him say, "It's okay now. You're safe. Now you can rest."

My Hero

The promotional testimony made a believer out of me. "That's what I want to do," I thought as I sat in my pew. It was all about Twixt, a church program to provide mentors for young boys desperate for a strong male influence.

I watched as sweet little boys between the ages of eight and twelve described what the Twixt program had meant in their lives. I could see the admiration in their eyes as they looked at the volunteers—men who took them to ball games and helped them with homework. Standing before me in my church were authentic, flesh-and-blood heroes.

That's what I wanted—to be some little boy's hero. I had two grown daughters; this would be my chance to have a son. I could see the two of us working on little arts-and-crafts projects, then flying together in my plane. Someday he would stand before the church, smiling up at me angelically as he said, "Ken Davis is my hero." I signed up right after church.

Several weeks later, all the volunteers were asked to attend a briefing. We learned about the children assigned to us and the responsibilities of being a Twixt partner. Many of the boys, we were told, had been abused or betrayed by their fathers. It could take some time to win their friendship and gain their trust. The boys had filled out questionnaires to help us get to know them before meeting face-to-face. We were to read the questionnaires and ask questions.

My face began to burn as I read my boy's folder. My dreams of an adoring little third-grader looking to me as a hero dissolved in fear. I'd been duped. My partner was two years older than the upper age limit of the program. The questionnaire had asked for his favorite sport; he'd scrawled, "None!"

What were his hobbies? "None."

What did he feel were his greatest strengths? "None."

My Twixt partner had answered only two questions. His name, he had confirmed, was Josh Blay; his favorite kind of music was "Death Metal." I didn't know what "Death Metal" was, but I didn't think they'd be playing it in our church on Sunday.

I was angry. "I thought these boys were looking for companionship," I protested. Anyone could tell this boy didn't want to be in the program. "You tease me with little boys still young enough to look up to an adult," I complained, "and you give me a teenage rebel. I haven't got the time, energy, or skills to meet this boy's needs."

The leader of the group explained that Josh's father had just been sent to prison for life. His mother was left to raise four children on her own; she desperately wanted a positive male influence for Josh. "We chose Josh as your partner," the chairwoman said, "because we thought you were the most qualified to be his friend."

Another one of the volunteers spoke up. "This isn't about your needs, Ken; it's about Josh's needs." He said it kindly, but the words stung. I wanted to snap back, "Then why don't *you* take him?"

Several weeks later, the church threw a party designed to allow us to meet our Twixt partners. Josh's questionnaire prepared me for a hulking, surly teenager with a bone through his nose and a bad disposition to match. Instead I was introduced to a small, shy boy who barely weighed a hundred pounds. I liked him instantly.

Josh didn't talk much even after we got to know each other. I did learn that he disliked church and wasn't very fond of talking about his relationship with God. I liked Josh because he was totally honest. He had a great sense of humor and a genuine desire to do the right thing. Over the period of a year I learned as much from Josh as he learned from me. There were no deep discussions, no heartwarming conversion experiences—just my growing love for a boy with wonderful potential.

My only disappointment was a perception that it was all one-way. I told Josh how much I'd grown to care about him. I shared my heart, my family, and my life with him—but Josh shared little with me. I wondered if any good could result from what seemed like a lopsided relationship.

One night as I was going to bed, the phone rang. It was Josh. "Can I come over and use your computer?" he asked. He was late writing a school report that was due the next day. Since Josh didn't drive, I'd have to get dressed, drive the fifteen minutes to his house, bring him back to my house, wait for him to finish the report, and then drive him back home. It was going to be a long night.

I brought Josh to my home, showed him how to use the computer, and left him to write his report. I told him I'd help him run a grammar and spelling check when he'd finished. About an hour later, Josh called me into the office to help him finish his report. I read the first three lines and burst into tears. Here is his report:

THE PERSON I ADMIRE

The person I admire is my mentor, Ken Davis. I respect him because he teaches me things that I didn't know. He teaches me to do better in school by giving me twenty dollars for every B. [He quickly cleaned up the Cs and Ds and cleaned out my wallet.] He takes me places that I haven't been before. He lets me fly his own plane. He thinks that I can do better than I think I can, if only I put my mind to it. Sometimes Ken helps me get jobs. He's always trying to help me and my family.

I've known him for two years. I met him though a church program that I didn't want to do, but my mom made me. But instead of telling the truth on the application, I put down all this satanic stuff so nobody would pick me as a mentor. When Ken got my slip he didn't want anything to do with me. He wasn't even going to meet me, so my plan almost worked. But now I'm glad that he stuck with the program.

Without him I don't think I would be doing as good as I am now. I would probably be doing bad in school and getting into a lot of trouble. He has a wife, Diane, and two daughters, Traci and Taryn. He is a motivational speaker. I might go with him to one of his out-of-state programs this summer.

In conclusion, I respect him for all the things he does and all the things he has taught me.

Josh Blay
Period 3
5–14–97

I equally admire Josh. In many ways he is a hero in my eyes. I'm not sure I'd have demonstrated such character and courage if I'd been placed in a situation like his. I have many hopes and dreams for Josh. Not the least of them is that he'll someday find the wisdom to totally trust the God who created him. I'm grateful for Josh's friendship. In his own way, Josh let me know that ours was not a one-way friendship. I did, after all, become a hero to someone—and he became a hero to me.

Don't believe the questionnaire. Beneath the outward appearance of rebellion, you'll often find gold just waiting to be mined and refined by someone willing to care—even an ordinary someone like you and me.

The LORD does not look at the things man looks at. Man looks at the outward appearance, but the LORD looks at the heart. —1 Samuel 16:7

Signs of the Times

Signs are designed to grab our attention. They alert us to danger or promote some product. Some signs, however, defy understanding. The following are signs found in real life:

On a bag of Fritos: "You could be a winner! No purchase necessary. Details inside."

On packaging for a Rowenta Iron: "Do not iron clothes on body."

On a Korean kitchen knife: "Warning. Keep out of children."

On an American Airlines packet of nuts: "Instructions: Open packet, eat nuts."

On a Swedish chain saw: "Do not attempt to stop chain with your hands."

As I write this, I'm sitting in the exit row of an airliner cruising at thirty thousand feet. In front of me is a briefing card with these words boldly printed on top: "If you are sitting in an exit row and you cannot read this card or cannot see well enough to follow these instructions, please tell a crew member." It seems to me that if I can't read or see well enough to read the instructions on the card, I'm going to have an awfully hard time following its instructions.

That's no worse than the large billboard you can see just before the exit to the Louisville Expo Center. It announces, "Tattoos while you wait." Excuse me, but isn't waiting a pretty solid requirement for getting a tattoo? "Tattoos on the go" are pretty much out of the question. I can't even conceive of "Tattoos while you jog."

And I've seen a jewelry store in Denver that promises to pierce ears "half off" on Thursdays. Uh . . . thanks but No Thanks!

Near our home is the highest paved road in the continental United States. Trail Ridge Road winds over a mountain pass at 12,183 feet. It takes my car two hours to struggle to the top. But I can see for hundreds of miles in every direction from the summit. Some overachiever employed by the State of Colorado—a true Master of the Obvious—has erected a huge sign at the summit. Here is the full text of that sign:

HILL

No lie! They've also included a picture of a hill, just in case you might mistake the next fifteen-mile luge ride as a large dip.

Speaking of dips, who decides the location of those signs? Usually it's only after peeling myself off the ceiling of the car that I see the "dip" sign. I feel strongly that a "dip" sign should be more of a warning than an acknowledgment. All these signs do is accurately describe the person who placed them there.

As a child I once saw a man on the street wearing a sandwich board. On his front sign, in large letters, were the words, "THE END IS NEAR!"

"What end?" I asked. "How near?"

The answer I received was chilling. There was no time to wait for tattoos or to get ears pierced half off. I was told that the cataclysmic demise of the earth was just around the corner. For several nights I lay awake wondering if those bumps and thumps in the darkness were the beginning of the end. I checked under my bed regularly to see if The End might be hiding there.

But the weeks rolled by and I awoke to one sunrise after another. In time, the power of the message faded into obscurity. I went back to living under the false assumption behind which most people cringe: *There is no end.*

No one knows exactly when the end will come, but the truth is printed on the rearview mirrors of every new car: "Objects in mirror may be closer than they appear." The Bible is clear that the end will come—and that it's nearer than we think. The man with the sandwich board has a healthy respect for the truth.

John Ortberg learned this valuable lesson from his grandmother. The genteel woman was a ruthless Monopoly player. She seemed unbeatable. But one day the young Ortberg prevailed. His enthusiastic celebration was interrupted by a lesson he never forgot. He was gloating over his victory, gleefully dragging all the property and money he'd won toward himself. His grandmother said, "Just remember, John: When the game is over, it all goes back in the box. The money, the hotels, the cars— everything goes back in the box."

My pastor detailed the parallel truth found in life: "A businessman with hotels and houses and a huge bank account feels a twinge in his chest as he finishes his morning jog—and in a heartbeat everything goes back in the box.

"A teenager slides behind the wheel of his new car. His girlfriend sits smiling beside him. An oncoming car crosses the centerline—and it all goes back in the box. When the game is over, we too go back in the box."

Everywhere we find signs that this life is not forever. If you don't believe the Bible, then look in the mirror. If you need more proof, conduct a search for anyone born two hundred years ago. Or take a quiet walk through a cemetery. History provides perfect evidence that the game will end. We can't pinpoint the precise time, but we know the end may be closer than it appears. At that time it won't matter what kind of career we've built, how many hotels we've accumulated, or what kind of cars we drove. It all goes back in the box. You never see a hearse pulling a U-Haul.

Just a thought:

Now that I'm fifty years closer to the end, the message seems less chilling. It's almost comforting. It serves as a reminder to concentrate on the things that are most important: my Lord, my children, and my wife. I'm more eager to make a difference in the lives of the people I touch. I'm more eager to spend time nurturing my relationship with Jesus Christ.

I think about one more little sign. This one used to hang on the wall in my Sunday school class. It read, "Only one life 'twill soon be past. Only what's done for Christ will last." Now that's a good sign!

The end of all things is near. Therefore be clear minded and self-controlled so that you can pray. Above all, love each other deeply, because love covers over a multitude of sins. —1 Peter 4:7–8

Is Sex a Four-Letter Word?

I learned about sex from my cousin. As we walked along a road, we were throwing stones at the birds lined up on the telephone wire. As you can tell, I didn't grow up in the inner city.

We eventually came to a field of cattle. There, right by the side of the road, a bull was breeding a cow. We rolled on the ground and laughed until I thought my sides would split. What was so funny? I admit it wasn't a pretty sight, but neither was it a high moment in comedy.

I imagine I was laughing to conceal that I felt confused and stupid. I grew up on a farm, so I'd seen these things before. But I'd never felt the need to laugh. For that matter, I'd assisted in the delivery of several calves. Deep down inside, those experiences had stirred questions about my own origins as well as my own sexuality. But believe it or not, until that day with my cousin, I'd never put two and two (or in this case, one and one) together. It was easier to laugh than to reveal my ignorance and risk ridicule.

After the bull had completed his performance and we'd exhausted all the crude comments we could think of, my cousin turned to me and said, "That's what your father did to your mother to get you."

I hit him in the face and he fell to the ground. I was right on top of him, pummeling with both fists. "Don't you ever say that about my mom and dad!" I shouted. He was laughing at me. And the more he insisted it was true, the madder I got. I'd always thought of sex as something crude and dirty. My parents weren't crude and dirty, nor were they cows. So how could he say they would do such a thing?

Before long, of course, I discovered my cousin was right—and at the same time quite wrong. He had the basic physiological facts down, but he knew nothing of the spiritual and emotional aspects of sex. I've spent the rest of my life undoing the distorted perspective of sex I received as an adolescent.

I've written thousands of words to teenagers concerning sexuality, yet it's obvious that many adults are just as confused as their kids in this sex-obsessed nation. I'm sure my experience is typical. I grew up believing that sex was something dirty—outside the realm of God. That misconception gave sex an allure and a power far beyond what God intended. It became "forbidden fruit."

We promote this image of sex by what we *don't* say to our kids. When we fail to talk about it, we might as well be handing the keys of our children's sex lives to strangers. Their friends, the media, and the purveyors of pornography will eagerly fill in the blanks, and the ideas they promote are nowhere near God's wonderful intention.

What our Creator had in mind was a wonderfully intimate expression of a deeper love. Yes! There is indeed a joy deeper than sex—the profound love of two people committed to each other until death. I'd be laughed off any TV talk show for making that statement; yet those doing the laughing would also be longing for the security and joy of such a relationship.

That kind of relationship requires work, commitment, and self-control. In light of the price we must pay, many people settle for cheap substitutes. I watch the couple across the street sit on the front porch holding hands. They've been married for seventy years. Their kind of love won't be featured on any TV shows this week. The media would be more fascinated by the life of my friend across town. He's a man with a posh bachelor pad. Each week a different woman decorates his life. At twenty-seven, in his more honest moments he admits to a deep loneliness beneath his machismo exterior.

In the movie *When Harry Met Sally*, there's a very funny scene in which an entire restaurant watches as Meg Ryan moans and groans in ecstasy. When she finishes her little charade, an elderly woman calls the waiter over and whispers, "I'll have whatever she's having." That happens with many of us. We watch the swingers and the sexually promiscuous, and, because we don't see the consequences, we think, "I'll have what they're having."

No thank you, I think I'll take whatever my elderly friends across the street are having. It must be good. It's lasted seventy years.

There's no denying the thrill of casual sexual encounter, but its intensity is short-lived. An intimate, committed relationship offers benefits that last a lifetime. That's where the best sex is found. That's the way God intended it.

Marital commitment is hard work. But if you're willing to do the heavy lifting in building relational intimacy, you'll find you've laid the foundation for sexual intimacy as well. God wants you to enjoy what he created. (Yes, I'm still talking about sex.)

Song of Songs, with all its sexual imagery, didn't slip into the Bible accidentally. It's part of the inspired Word of God, and without embarrassment it proclaims the beauty of sex. It's a pity we don't hear many sermons preached from the Song of Songs.

Just a thought:

Obviously sex doesn't embarrass God. He isn't prudish about it, and he never asked us to be so. Look into his perspective on sex—you may be surprised. Follow his guidelines, and you'll be amazed at the character and faith a godly approach to sex can build.

Let your children know that sex is a creation of God. Teach them that the most powerful enjoyment of sex comes not from responding to every glandular stimulus, but by lifting sex to the place of honor it deserves.

It's Easy!

I remember the day my friend in California asked me to go surfing with him. "I don't know how," I responded.

"Oh, it's easy!" he laughed. "Just tie this board to your foot, paddle out, wait for the Big One, and ride it in!"

Who was I to argue? So I attached a bungee cord to my ankle. This is something you do so that when you plummet into the pounding surf, you don't have to swim to shore to get your surfboard. It stays right there with you and beats your body to a bleeding pulp.

My next instruction was to paddle out and wait for the Big One. Of course I had no idea what the Big One was. The only big thing that came to my mind as I stood gazing at the crashing surf was that thumping musical theme from *Jaws*. If the Big One was some great fishy predator with razor blades for teeth, then he could ride himself in. I started to untie the bungee cord.

My tanned, muscular friend, smiling with his own impressive teeth, convinced me there were no sharks. He and I paddled out into the deep and waited for the Big One. A few nice swells actually slipped beneath our boards, lifting us toward the sky. "Not bad," I thought. "I can handle this."

Suddenly a strong undertow began to suck us out toward the open sea. I turned just in time to see a great, watery skyscraper bearing down on us. It was just like one of those waves you saw on *Hawaii Five-O*, foam whipping from the top, the curl poising to crash down. So this was the Big One!

I did not ride the Big One. The Big One rode me. I found myself churning head over heels, thirty feet underwater, praying for little things like . . . air. Somehow I made it to the surface, only to be pummeled by thundering surf. I spent the next ten minutes dodging a twenty-pound board attached to my body with a big rubber band.

I moved to Minnesota and bought a house on a lake. No surf.

I'd lived in Minnesota only a few days when some friends invited us over to water-ski. "I don't know how," I said.

"Oh, it's easy!" my friend replied. "Just stand here on shore, hold on tight to this stick, and yell, 'Hit it!'"

Why didn't he tell me about letting slack out of the rope first?

The boat was going full tilt as the last bit of slack whistled from the rope coiled at my feet. I was still standing on shore, but it felt like my arms had been ripped out of their sockets and were flopping behind the boat still holding the stick in a death grip. I finally did manage to ski, but it wasn't easy. Why didn't my friend tell me, "When you fall, let go of the rope"?

I fell and held on for dear life. They trolled half the lake with me. I'm sure the fish had never seen such a large lure in all their life. Thank heaven we weren't skiing in *Jaws* territory.

Suddenly my swimming trunks were torn from my body. I let go of the stick and lunged to retrieve them. Now I was praying for two things: air and clothing. As I popped up to the surface gasping for air, I saw something that terrified me. A boat full of my friends was coming back to pick me up. I didn't want to be picked up; I was naked. Even the fish had gathered in groups. I could almost hear them: "Oh, that's gross! Get him out of here!"

I frantically waved the boat away, telling them I wanted to swim to shore. I got there exhausted, then realized I had a problem: I still had no swimming suit. I gathered some seaweed, sticks, and leaves and made a run for the boathouse. Little children were yelling, "Mommy, Mommy, it's Adam, it's Adam!"

So I moved to Colorado. Within a week, someone said, "Let's go skiing."

"I don't know how," I said.

He said, "It's easy!"

I said, "Eat rocks."

I'd heard enough about *easy*. Nothing worth having is easy. Diane and I recently celebrated our thirtieth wedding anniversary—and every minute has been worth it. But it hasn't been easy. We raised two daughters who have grown up to be responsible and delightful adults. It was worth it! But it wasn't easy.

Being a follower of Jesus has not always been easy, but I wouldn't trade one second of my walk with him for an easier way without him. When we believe the lie that says "it's easy," we end up with little more than guilt and discouragement. If skiing doesn't come easy, you may feel unqualified and give up. If marriage doesn't come easy, you may feel like you're failing. You may even feel justified in throwing in the towel.

Well, don't give up! Every worthy venture in life is filled with obstacles. Every thriving relationship crosses dark valleys of doubt. The freedoms we enjoy in this great country were purchased with the blood and sweat of millions of men and women. The word *easy* didn't apply.

Ask the men who followed Jesus Christ if following him was easy. They paid for their devotion with their lives. The price paid for your forgiveness didn't come easy—even for the Son of God.

Does your life include struggles and temptations and difficulty? Take heart. You're in good company. Difficulty is not a sign you're doing something wrong; it's a sign you're alive. If someone stands before you with an easy promise of wealth or health or achievement—RUN. Only being dead is easy.

Just a thought:

Rarely do I watch late-night television, but a few nights ago I was doing some midnight surfing—this time with a remote. I stopped momentarily on a channel where a young man sat in a beautiful convertible parked on a dock next to his yacht. He was holding a fistful of money as he instructed the camera to show a panorama of his palatial summer home.

"In the next thirty minutes," he lied, "I'll show you how you can be a millionaire just like me. It's easy."

"Eat rocks," I said out loud as I banished him from my living room with a click of the remote control. Now that was easy.

I have told you these things, so that in me you may have peace. In this world you will have trouble. But take heart! I have overcome the world.
—*John 16:33*

Hit It Straight— Finish Well

It seemed like a good idea to teach my wife the game of golf. I even made it easy for her by allowing her to pick up her errant shot and hit again from where *my* ball had landed. But teaching her to golf turned out to be one of the biggest mistakes I ever made. Now Diane beats me on a consistent basis. Her drives only carry about 180 yards, but each one goes straight down the fairway. My drives carry about 230 yards, but they go where no man has ever gone before. While I'm wrestling an alligator or rooting around for my ball in the rose garden of an indignant homeowner, Diane is calmly driving her next shot another hundred yards right down the middle of the fairway.

I hit the ball with a sharp smack, usually accompanied by a loud grunt and a desperate flailing to stay on my feet. Then I'm yelling "Fore!" to help innocent bystanders stay on *their* feet. "Fore!" is what you yell to warn people you've hit an errant ball capable of injuring them. I yell "Fore!" quite often. Diane predicts I'll kill somebody one day. She may be right.

I see golf tournaments on television. If crowds were to line up on each side of the fairway like that when I play, someone would die. Fans would learn to quickly hit the turf when they saw me step to the tee. When Diane steps up to the fairway, there are no grunts or mutterings—just a kind of ho-hum swing followed by a straight-arrow arc, headed for the green.

I lined up on a wide, beautiful fairway not too long ago. I thought to myself, "I can't miss!" The only hazard was a tiny pond about fifty yards directly to my left. I went through all the little pre-shot wiggles and hitches I've picked up from the pros: Wiggle the rear. Wiggle the toes. Wiggle the club. Hitch the pants. Touch the cap.

I took a mighty swing. The ball hit the heel of the club and careened at a ninety-degree angle from the intended destination. With a sickening *kerplunk* it disappeared into the tiny pond.

I had violated several laws of physics. The pond was almost at my back. I teed up another ball, wiggled everything appropriate, and let 'er rip. Once again, the ball hit the edge of my club and shot directly sideways into the little pond. Muttering under my breath (spiritual things, of course), I teed up a third ball. I wouldn't let it happen again. I was not stupid.

If the ball insisted on going directly to the left, fine! I would adjust my strategy. Surely if I aimed at the beautiful homes to my right, the ball would hang its usual left and end up somewhere in the fairway. I lined it up and swung with all my might. The ball hit the same edge of my club, ricocheted off my heel and went into the same stupid little pond.

Diane walked up and whispered sweetly, "Perhaps you should use an old ball."

"I don't have an old ball," I snapped. "I've never been able to keep a ball long enough for it to get old."

"Why don't you just come up to where my ball is, drop another ball, and start from there," she suggested. She had no idea how humiliating that would be. I would rather hit three more into the water. She's so consistent and so methodical; I'm so macho and so wild.

My practice swings are perfect. They're relaxed and without strain. "Relax," I say as I set up in front of the ball. "Keep it smooth," I think as I swing the club back. "Nice and easy, like Diane," I think as my club reaches the top of my backswing. I will hesitate before swinging the club smoothly through the ball.

"NOW—KILL IT!"

Some demon roars as the club begins its descent. Every muscle tenses, my eyeballs bulge out, a grunt escapes my lips, and the ball sails toward some innocent driver on a nearby freeway.

Diane's golf game is like her life: quiet, consistent, and steady. Every morning she gets up at 7:00 A.M. and goes for a walk. A walk? Who can get into shape going for a walk? I'm a runner. Every month or so I rise early and go for a run—five or six miles, after which I spend five or six weeks recuperating.

You know what? I don't think God is looking for the macho types. I think he is looking for the steady types. The world is full of quick starters, those with a mighty swing and a limp follow-through. It's those like my beautiful wife who win out. While I'm swinging as hard as I can from deep in the forest, she's quietly pressing on toward the goal. While I'm running my five miles once a month, she's walking five miles each day. God isn't looking for people who can sprint fast or hit hard—he's looking for people who will cross the finish line and who will make it to the green.

If you can't hit the ball as far as the person in front of you, don't be discouraged. If the other runners seem to be passing you before you finish the first lap, don't give up. The prize doesn't go to the one who gets out of the blocks first. The prize goes to the one who finishes.

Let us fix our eyes on Jesus, the author and perfecter of our faith, who for the joy set before him endured the cross, scorning its shame, and sat down at the right hand of the throne of God. Consider him who endured such opposition from sinful men, so that you will not grow weary and lose heart.
—Hebrews 12:2–3

Alive and Screaming Clean

For Traci and Taryn, camping in the wilderness was a big part of growing up. We took them on long trips that taught big lessons and provided warm memories.

We didn't use campgrounds with running water, communal bathrooms, and a camp store—we went deep into the wilderness, miles from any road or sign of civilization. We carried the camp store on our backs. The girls wore small backpacks while Diane and I carried large, overloaded packs filled with enough stuff to supply a small country.

We always tried to camp near a crystal-clear stream for drinking water. Bathing in it took hours—a few seconds for the actual bath, a few hours to work up the courage to touch that frigid, icy washcloth to the skin. That process would trigger a ritualistic dance that must have fascinated the animals.

But the hardest part loomed ahead: the rinse. The rinse involved pouring a pan of the ice-cold stream water over my body until all the biodegradable soap was gone. This act would make even a Southern Baptist dance. It was so awful that everyone but me skipped it. They would walk around with a thick residue of biodegradable soap on their bodies. We always knew when someone was rinsing because of the scream. I never screamed, but I sucked in enough air to cause an oxygen shortage on the mountain for several days.

The girls in our family (that is, everyone but me) hated high-country bathing—partly because they didn't like near-death experiences, but mostly because of the modesty factor. "Deer and elk aren't like humans," I insisted. "They don't care. And if a squirrel happens to catch a glimpse of your goose-bumpy body dancing at the edge of a stream, so what? Who's he going to tell?"

"Maybe that's what they're always chattering about," Diane chimed in.

I've lived long enough with three women to know there was no logical argument to win them over. Any hope I ever had of doing so was destroyed a few days later. The girls were refusing to bathe unless I secured an area the size of Texas and stood guard with a weapon. I argued that in all our years of camping, we'd always enjoyed perfect privacy. Never had a friend or relative dropped by and said, "Hi, how are you?" during a stream bath.

I finally gave up. Exhausted from a day of hiking and tired of arguing, I walked several hundred yards from camp to take my own bath. I knew a place where a beautiful stream ran just at the edge of a high mountain meadow. The view was breathtaking. Perched at eleven thousand feet, the sun-drenched meadow sloped down and away from the stream to a blue-green valley miles below. I could see for a hundred miles. A game-trail skirted the edge of the meadow and disappeared into the forest in front of me.

I took my bath in the midst of this splendor and braced myself for the rinse. Covered only with shampoo and soap and standing ankle-deep in the stream, I closed my eyes and dumped a large pan of freezing water over my body. I whooped with exhilaration, scooped up another pan of water—and heard the unmistakable snort of a horse.

My eyes flew open. Ten horses had emerged from the forest and were walking past me on the trail not thirty yards away. I couldn't run; bare feet are incompatible with sharp rocks and broken sticks. I couldn't hide; the water was too shallow. I could only stand sheepishly as ten riders stared off into the valley pretending they'd seen nothing out of the ordinary.

But I knew different. I was close enough to see their shoulders shaking with laughter, and I could see the fear in the horses' eyes. As they disappeared into the forest on the other side of the meadow, the last rider turned and waved. I couldn't wave back. I was using both hands to strategically position the washcloth. I only prayed that I'd never meet any of these people again.

I made the mistake of telling my family. From then on, the girls and Diane bathed with their clothes on.

Horses, riders, and humor aside, for me there are few moments in life more exhilarating than those moments of standing clean and refreshed in the unspoiled beauty of God's creation. I think a combination of factors accounts for that feeling.

First, it feels so good to be clean—to know that the sweat and grime of the day are gone.

Second, it feels so good to be alive. Trust me: If you have any doubts that you're alive, a quick dip in a snow-fed stream will convince you.

The sound of your screams tumbling down the mountain will convince every other living thing too.

Third, it's so thrilling to stand in the midst of so much evidence that God is alive. There's an awesome power and an unspoiled innocence about the wilderness. Being there persuades me that the Creator intended for our lives to be that spotless and that spectacular. God knew what he was doing when he designed mountain streams. His Son called the forgiveness he offers us "living water."

You may never have the chance to taste the water gushing from a spring at ten thousand feet. You may never stand in a pure, ice-cold stream totally refreshed and clean, every nerve tingling with life, praying that the horseys will stay away. You may never see the majesty of his creation from a rocky mountaintop.

But you can experience all of this in even greater measure. When you drink of the forgiveness God offers, you'll know the refreshment of being totally clean. No mountain stream can match it. When you discover the hope and purpose he brings to your life, every nerve in your body comes alive. No thrill equals the thrill of knowing his purpose for life. When your eyes are open to the wonders he brings to pass in the human heart, you'll rejoice that he is alive.

Just a thought:

Dive in and be cleansed; drink deeply and live.

For the Lamb at the center of the throne will be their shepherd; he will lead them to springs of living water. And God will wipe away every tear from their eyes. —Revelation 7:17

Don't Give Up

"Parenting is easy." That's what a well-known author told several thousand mothers of preschool children. Then I listened as he laid out Three Easy Steps to Being a Great Parent. Each step included an illustration from his own life, detailing how he'd applied the steps to become a Great Parent himself.

Public speaking is a privilege, and it carries with it a responsibility to be honest. This speaker didn't intentionally lie—but he lied. He implied that following his easy steps could get these moms through the messy quagmire of parenting.

Yeah, right.

When struggling parents read or hear this kind of thing, they begin to see themselves as failures. I studied the sea of tired but hopeful faces that day, and I wondered how many of them would simply become more discouraged. How many would rediscover that there are no easy steps to parenting? I wondered how many felt singled out as poor parents because it wasn't as easy for them as it was for the Perfect Parent on the platform. The same deception has occurred at marriage and discipleship seminars.

Parenting is about relationships, and nothing involving relationships is easy. Relationships require constant work—and failure is built into the process. For example, children are constantly changing mentally and physically. Keeping pace with those changes is tough. Today they need a diaper; tomorrow it's the keys to the car. One day they depend on you, and the next they're ashamed of you. Children can give you a brief glimpse of hell as they navigate the treacherous waters of adolescence.

No, it's not easy being a good parent. In fact, it sometimes seems impossible. Why pretend otherwise?

I was totally shocked when a couple that seemed to have a perfect marriage suddenly plunged into a bitter divorce. They appeared to have no problems—which turned out to be the problem, as I later discovered. They had many problems. Rather than deal with them, they decided to focus on a public portrayal of perfection. They ignored reality until their pretense grew impossible to maintain. Their marriage was destroyed because they refused to acknowledge and address the real issues.

After one of my programs in Orlando, two old friends approached me. Doug and Donna had been active in my Sunday-school class twenty-five years before. As we renewed acquaintances, they recalled all our happy experiences—and all the struggles of their marriage. These two fought battles visible to those surrounding them. They argued in our class meetings and aired out their marital problems.

Now, years later, Doug looked me in the eye and said, "Remember how troubled our marriage used to be? We almost called it quits several times over the years. But God has helped heal our relationship. It's not perfect, but it's better than ever before." He put his arm around Donna and beamed. "We're going to make it."

I wanted to jump up and down. Someone was telling the truth! Finally, a testimony I could believe, one that would give struggling couples a ray of hope. It was refreshing to hear observations from real people about a real God.

Great authors and speakers—even twisted people like myself—may occasionally give helpful advice. But no matter how famous the writer or speaker may be, when you see or hear the words "three easy steps"—RUN! Skip to the next page, or at least take a pen and scratch out the word "easy."

When you begin to feel like a failure in light of the wisdom and perfection of some expert—STOP! List all the problems you face and take them to the guru. If the guru is honest, he'll admit to facing many of the same problems and often failing in the process of living them.

I don't learn much from people who have it all together, for no one has it all together. I learn best from people who admit they're not okay, have the courage to face the specific areas in which they're not okay, and are working toward *making* it okay. Honest people never make it their aim to leave their listeners feeling, "I wish I could be like that person." Honest people want to ignite their listeners with this hope: "If God can help that person—an authentic, flawed human being—then surely God can help me."

In light of the above, here are three easy . . . Scratch that! How about a few suggestions from someone who struggles just like you do?

Don't give up. You're not the only person facing those problems and temptations. Millions of people are coping with them daily and trusting God for a way to make tomorrow better. You may not have the strength to face all of it alone—but you don't have to. The Creator of the universe wants to come alongside you with supernatural power that can make a difference.

No temptation has seized you except what is common to man. And God is faithful; he will not let you be tempted beyond what you can bear. But when you are tempted, he will also provide a way out so that you can stand up under it. —1 Corinthians 10:13

Don't give in. Misery loves company. Once we recognize that everyone faces the same kinds of problems, there may be a temptation to simply give up and wallow in our misery, to settle for the status quo. In any situation, there are only two options: to work to make the situation better or to watch the situation grow worse. To decide not to do anything is a decision to make the situation worse.

What shall we say, then? Shall we go on sinning so that grace may increase? By no means! We died to sin; how can we live in it any longer? —Romans 6:1–2

Don't go it alone. Fellow strugglers are all around you. Find some friends who are committed to being better parents, better spouses, and better Christians; work together to make tomorrow better than today.

Therefore encourage one another and build each other up, just as in fact you are doing. —1 Thessalonians 5:11

Part 2: Living Life

*Blessed are those who have learned to acclaim you, who walk in the light of your presence, O L*ORD.   —*Psalm 89:15*

Air Bags, Seat Belts, and Change

Ready for the day, I unbuckled my seat belt. I knelt on the front seat, bent over into the backseat, and began rummaging in the great junk-heap that constitutes the floor of my car.

I was desperately seeking my daily planner, which I often toss into the backseat rather than lugging it into the house. Without that book, sheer chaos was certain. I hadn't a clue where I was supposed to be or whom to call to find out where I was supposed to be. I didn't know what to do—my To-Do list was in the book. Everything was in the book. Without the book, my very existence could be called into question.

I was totally absorbed in rummaging through the artifacts on the floor. Half-eaten pizza, Happy-Meal boxes, and sticky Dairy-Queen cups flew in every direction. Did you know that if your face is on the carpet, your car can be accelerating down the street without your knowledge or permission? I didn't know that either.

I'd accidentally left the vehicle in gear. My head was buried in the backseat, and my own back seat was elevated to headrest position. That sector of my anatomy, it should be noted, is sight-impaired.

I found the planner! Still facing backwards, I popped up with a victorious smirk. Then I noticed from the corner of my eye that various objects seemed to be moving slowly past the side window. Suddenly it hit me: My car was rolling! I spun quickly to stop the car, but a lamppost beat me to it.

Have you ever had your air bag go off?

I have, and I'm here to tell you it's nothing like TV commercials would have you believe. Those commercials present the air bag as something you'd activate purely for the entertainment value, like playing with a giant, undulating marshmallow. Hollywood's special-effects wizards create this illusion by showing the deployment of the air bag in superslow motion. Your kids beg you for a try. It looks like a great new ride for the amusement park.

My air bag wasn't even remotely like that. The slow motion must have been out of order. I didn't hear it coming, I didn't see it coming; it was just suddenly there. *Whap*! I had no idea what happened. All I knew was that my nose hurt worse than it had ever hurt in my life.

If I were designing cars, I'd install some kind of warning system. Perhaps one of those synthetic voices: "Your air bag is set to deploy in ten seconds," it would intone calmly. "We suggest you get out of the car."

After the air bag hit me, I kept my eyes closed for ten minutes. I had no choice in the matter—my glasses were embedded in my head. And I still had no clue what had happened. The car was full of powder and the air bag had deflated. Through my tears, I only wondered why a huge hanky was now hanging from my steering wheel.

A bad word formed in the back of my head, stood up, and began making its way through the aisles and hallways of my brain, all the way to the front office where the lips are. Yes, it seemed almost certain I'd be starting my day with a curse. Now, I know what some of you are thinking: "No way! How could an inspirational author have a swearword in his head?"

Because I'm human, that's how. I still haven't reached that point in my pilgrimage where Scriptures come to my lips whenever my nose is broken. And my best guess is that you haven't either. If I were to suddenly reach out of this book and punch you in the nose, I doubt your reflex response would be, "Praise the Lord! I just want to thank God for your dynamic fist!"

If it's any comfort to you, the word in question never crossed the threshold of my lips. Before it came out, I started to laugh. I laughed until I cried. Why not? The tears were already there. For some reason, the phrase *air bag* took hold of me: What a ridiculous term! Twenty years ago no such phrase existed. Had I driven a car home and told my mother I had an air bag in my car, she would have responded in horror: "That's not a kind thing to say!"

How things change. What didn't exist yesterday is a household word today. As I laughed, my mind began to run free. (Don't worry; it has no air bags.) I began to laugh at my seat belt. When I was a child, there was no such term as "seat belt" either. My mother was the safety device in our car. If I wanted to stand on the front seat, perch on the headrest, or drool out the window like our dog—no problem. In the event of an accident, my mother would save me with her arm.

Actually, it didn't require an accident. Whenever she hit the brake, her arm would simultaneously arc toward me like a loose boom on a sailing ship: *Whap!* Talk about your tough love. "Why'd ya do that?" I'd snort through my bleeding nose.

"I kept you from going through the windshield," she'd reply with a look of heroic satisfaction.

"Can I go through the windshield next time?" I'd beg, still nursing my bleeding nose and sporting a shiner I'd never be able to explain to my friends. Very few kids, I believed, had ever died going through a windshield; but I suspected thousands were victims of the long arm of the mom.

That's exactly why I loved riding with my grandma. She had that *thing* under her arm—that fleshy, soft forerunner to the air bag thing. When Grandma stepped on the brakes, her arm would come flying back and I'd be smothered in gelatinous flesh. Everything would go black, and air would temporarily be cut off. But I didn't get hurt. Oh, I'd smell like Noxzema for a few days, but I could live with that.

My point is that nothing stays the same; everything changes. Grandma is no longer with us. If I understand heaven correctly, she no longer has the natural air bag. Automobiles have air bags, side-impact air bags, and switches for disengaging air bags. Parents are required to use infant seats to restrain children in cars. In my day, an infant seat was something you put a diaper on.

Change is everywhere. And it's picking up speed. Once-illegal actions are now commonplace. Laws that once protected the innocent now protect the guilty. Items once treasured are now discarded as worthless.

Even things that are dear to us change. Grandmas and grandpas die. Friends move away. The stock market falls. An auto accident suddenly removes a loved one we counted on to be there always. Sometimes it feels as if everything I thought dependable is slowly disappearing like a ship sinking beneath the waves. It's as if I'm afloat in a sea of change. Each piece of wreckage to which I cling has limited buoyancy and soon sinks, forcing me to hold tightly to another and then another.

Seeing so many things pass away, I've concluded there's little in this life I can count on for tomorrow. Only an unchanging God remains; he will never fail.

God is our refuge and strength, an ever-present help in trouble. There-fore we will not fear, though the earth give way and the mountains fall into the heart of the sea. . . . The LORD Almighty is with us; the God of Jacob is our fortress.   —Psalm 46:1–2, 11

Grab hold. Hang on. Don't let go.

Opportunity Knocks . . . But Not Always at the Front Door

I broke out in a cold sweat. I would be speaking to five hundred managers of a Fortune 500 company only ten minutes from now—and my notes were still in my hotel room on the ninth floor. I sprinted to the elevator, diving like Indiana Jones through the doors just as they closed. Whirling to face the front, I frantically pressed the button for the ninth floor. Then I crouched, panting like some predatory cat, poised to spring through the doors the second they opened.

A glance at my watch showed there were now seven minutes before speech time. The elevator finally reached the ninth floor and stopped. But the door didn't open. There was a sound like the door had opened. There was that little convulsive shake an elevator makes when the door opens. But the door didn't open. In a matter of moments, in a ballroom nine floors below me, I'd be introduced as the speaker. I could picture the applause, then the silence, the murmuring, and the confusion as no one came forward and stepped to the platform.

My imagination went wild. What if I was trapped in here for weeks? Maybe archaeologists would pry the door open sometime in the future, only to find my skeleton slumped in a corner. In a panic I pressed the little "Open Door" button. Each time I pressed, the elevator would make a sound as if the door were opening. It would shake as if the door were opening. But that door didn't open.

The bad word that had tried to escape my lips the day my air bag went off made it all the way this time. I kicked the door. I didn't want to hurt it; I wasn't trying to be destructive. I was only helping the maintenance people—I figured a good kick might jar the door loose. Maybe a second kick, a really good one, would be even more helpful.

In the process of abusing the door, I allowed my finger to slip from the little "Open Door" button and the elevator set off on its travels again.

Now I was frantic. The elevator crawled to the fourteenth floor and stopped. Once again it offered all the sound effects and tremors that accompany an opening door, and once again the door remained shut. I lost control. The clock was ticking—three minutes were left to avoid public humiliation before the tycoons of the world. I was ruined! I banged on the door, jabbed at the "Open Door" button, and started yelling, "Someone call the front desk! Call the police! The elevator door is stuck!"

From behind me, a timid voice squeaked, "No it ain't."

I felt a cold chill. The elevator had been empty when I entered it. Was the thing haunted? Every hair on my body stood at attention.

With bulging eyes I spun around, prepared to defend myself against some misty elevator phantom—only to face seven wide-eyed hotel guests waiting to get on.

This was one of those elevators with doors in both the front and the back. The people just stood there. They seemed reluctant to share a small, closed-in space with me.

The meeting had run long and I arrived at the ballroom in plenty of time for my speech. I recounted my ordeal as an illustration of how often we allow daily frustrations to affect our attitude. After the meeting a sweet elderly woman drew me aside. "I was standing there waiting to get on when the elevator stopped the first time," she said. Then with a wry smile, she shook her finger at me and clucked, "That *was* a bad word!"

I've recalled that incident many times. I've been on this ride before. Many times I've stood kicking at one door, screaming because it wouldn't open. I often fail to see open doors of opportunity all around me—doors leading to thrilling new destinations—because I want what I want, I want to get to it my way, and I want it now. The opportunity for me to get to my meeting was there all along, but I had my back turned. *I was beating on the wrong door.*

How often are we blinded to the opportunities God gives us because of our tunnel vision? I'm finally learning to look around for new doorways. It's never too late to open your eyes.

It could even keep you from saying some bad words.

Just a thought:

Is there a door you've tried to open that remains shut in spite of your best efforts? Have you taken a look around for alternate doors? The path to your dreams may be at the back of the elevator, the side of the elevator—even right through the roof. It may require more effort than you thought. Maybe you'll have to take the stairs instead.

Ask friends you trust if they see any open doors. God doesn't deprive us of opportunities, but narrow vision can blind us to what he's prepared for us. Ask God to show you the doors he has opened. There is nothing to lose by considering all your options. Lighten up and check the back door. You may be surprised at what you see.

Love in a Vacuum

I was settled deeply into my overstuffed armchair—so deeply I'd have to plan ahead in order to get out. This was my territory. I was a hard-working traveler, entertaining and inspiring people all over the world. I deserved this chair, this newspaper, these few precious, lazy moments. I looked up from my crossword puzzle, groping for a three-letter word starting with O, ending with D, and meaning "not young."

That's when I saw it. The door to the storage closet was slightly ajar. A solitary figure stood in its dim interior like a silent sentry from another planet. It sized me up with a robotic smirk. It was my old adversary—the vacuum cleaner.

My mind raced back to the day I bought the machine. I've always been a sucker for sales demonstrations. When I go to outdoor sporting shows, you can always find me standing in a trance, handing my money to some pitchman. I'll buy magnesium fire starters that ignite blazing campfires in hurricanes. Or a hand-cranked vegetable compactor/combination food dehydrator that makes peanut butter out of recycled zucchini skins. And that pocket-fisherman thing, as seen on TV. Fished around in my pocket for years. Never caught a thing.

The vacuum cleaner guy who appeared at our door that day must have thought he'd died and gone to heaven. I sat breathless as he demonstrated how the powerful suction of his vacuum cleaner could rip a newspaper to shreds. Then he leaned closer and lowered his voice: "You won't believe this," he said, as he reconfigured the vacuum cleaner so that it blew air out rather than sucking it in.

He pointed the nozzle of the hose upward and placed a Ping-Pong ball in the column of air rising from the machine. The ball bounced happily up and down, suspended in the airflow. I couldn't even speak. Then he whispered, "Watch this!"

From his little demonstration case he pulled a golf ball, which he released into the flow. This heavier ball dropped almost to the hose's nozzle before it began to bounce and bob in the column of air. I barely heard the salesman who looked over his shoulder as if to tell me a secret no one else could hear. He whispered, "Other vacuum cleaners won't do a golf ball!"

I was already reaching for my wallet. I paid over three hundred dollars for that vacuum cleaner, and to this day it won't suck dirt.

Now it fixed me with its metallic glare from the storage closet. I hadn't touched the thing since the salesman left. Oh, yes, I did entertain some friends with the Ping-Pong ball trick. But that was the extent of my vacuum cleaner experience.

In fact, that was about the extent of the housecleaning I offered my wife. Call me a recovering jerk. For the first fifteen years of my marriage, I was a terrible husband. Lazy and selfish, I'd determined that housework was women's work. Diane held down a full-time job to augment my income as a traveling speaker. She was my personal secretary, an attentive mother to our daughters, and she waited on me hand and foot without ever demanding that I lift a finger to help her.

I loved my wife very much, but I hadn't yet learned how to show my love. Our personal relationship was suffering from my insensitivity. With all the subtlety of a Neanderthal cave dweller I made brutish sexual advances, believing that was how a real man expressed love. It's no wonder that the physical passion and spiritual intimacy of our marriage had cooled considerably.

Oaf that I was, I couldn't figure out why she didn't respond to me. I believed my actions were sexy and attractive—why wasn't she falling all over me? Wasn't she grateful? Of all the women I could have married, I'd chosen her. I still spoke the words, "I love you," but she no longer responded with loving looks and tender embraces.

I was clueless. I had a lesson to learn about love, and God was going to use a vacuum cleaner to teach it.

As I stared at the three-hundred-dollar rug-sucker from the depths of my armchair, I was suddenly overcome with an overwhelming desire to vacuum. With considerable floundering, I extracted myself from the cushions and shuffled to the closet.

I learned many things about vacuuming that day. First, I learned that our cat was terrified of vacuum cleaners. That kept me entertained for about an hour.

I also discovered that vacuum cleaners are basically useless. They won't pick up important things. No matter how many times I ran the vacuum over a toothpick or a burr, it wouldn't pick it up. It would only embed it deeper into the carpet. Nor would it pick up rubber bands. Even with a stealthy approach, the brush on the vacuum would fling the rubber band across the room. I felt like a fool creeping around my own house, trying to sneak up on a rubber band.

The vacuum would pick up a piece of lint, hold it for an indiscriminate amount of time, then spit it back out when I least expected it.

I finally gave up, took the hose off the vacuum cleaner, left it running in the middle of the room, and brought stuff to it. The toothpicks, burrs, and other trash I fed it were snatched from my fingers, disappearing forever in the bowels of the monster, which hissed, "Mooooore! Moooooooooooore!"

When I could find no other visible trash, I replaced the hose and began to vacuum in earnest. That's when I discovered the stripes. As I vacuumed in one direction, a stripe would appear. Going the opposite direction would create a stripe of a different shade. Entranced, I striped the whole room. Then I went crossways, creating a checkerboard pattern.

I got so carried away that I dusted the furniture and straightened the entire house.

I was once again embedded in the easy chair, working on my crossword puzzle, when Diane came home. She struggled through the door with a bag of groceries under each arm, kicked the door shut with one foot, then took in the house with an expert glance.

Her mouth dropped open. Slowly the bags slipped from her grasp and dropped to the floor. "Who did this?" she asked.

"I did," I said, matter-of-factly.

Without warning, she attacked. Diving on me before I could get out of the chair, she smothered me with kisses and hugs, showering gratitude on me for helping her. The kisses grew more passionate. We broke the chair.

It was wonderful!

The vacuum cleaner taught me some important lessons that day. Love is expressed with more than just words. A husband's willingness to share the burdens of homemaking shouts "I love you" to his wife. After almost thirty years of marriage, I still have a lot to learn; but I could never treat my wife as I did back then.

It takes action to bring the words "I love you" to life. An unexpected card or a bouquet of flowers says, "I love you." Picking up after myself, cooking, or simply squeezing the toothpaste from the bottom of the tube says, "I love you."

This behavior brought pleasure to my wife, but there were other wonderful benefits. The physical passion returned to our marriage with an intensity I hadn't experienced for years. I've learned my lesson. I keep a Dustbuster with me everywhere we go!

Just a thought:

Isn't it amazing how little time we devote to making the world better for those around us? The expression of love goes far beyond just bringing home the bacon or providing the essentials of life. Love is expressed in the little things we do. Try each day to find some simple way to express your love for your spouse. Flowers? A card? A handwritten note? A date? Doing a chore you usually don't do? Breakfast in bed?

Personally I recommend vacuuming!

A new command I give you: Love one another. As I have loved you, so you must love one another. By this all men will know that you are my disciples, if you love one another. —John 13:34–35

Going First Class

Finally! I was headed for the big time. I'd collected enough frequent-flyer miles to earn a first-class upgrade. My seat was guaranteed, and I planned on making the most of it.

First class! I'd gazed wistfully upon it many times while boarding planes. It was the place where they helped you hang up your coat. It was where they offered you a beverage before takeoff. First class was the wonderful land of extra space, with room for extravagant carry-on items such as your legs. None of the flight attendants in first class were on parole. And now it was my turn to revel in the perks. Often, while passing through first class, I'd seen well-dressed people glance up from fine literature and corporate reports to smile knowingly. They knew I was headed for coach.

Coach. That's where the menu is always reconstituted leftovers from first class, with a side dish of unclassified vegetables. In coach, the line waiting to get into the rest room exceeds the number of passengers that boarded the plane. The seats are so close together that digging for your seat belt could result in a sexual harassment suit.

Coach is where the word "snack" is synonymous with six salted peanuts hermetically sealed in a swollen metallic/plastic bag that is impenetrable without power tools. I once watched a man's journey from sanity to incoherent babbling as he tried to open the peanut bag. I'd have offered him a knife, but mine had been confiscated at the security checkpoint. They'd never have taken it if I'd been traveling first class, but coach passengers aren't allowed to have sharp objects on their persons. We might conceivably use a knife to amputate a leg after gangrene sets in due to lack of blood flow.

But none of that today—I was going to fly in style. I was going first class. I woke up early and took a shower. First-class people always look like they've just showered. I put on my best suit and left early enough to pick up a copy of *Forbes* magazine and a book titled *Macho*

Management in a Micro Society—first-class literature, don't you know. I had no intention of looking like a visitor.

As I got on the plane, I handed my coat to the flight attendant and ordered a tomato juice with one cube of ice. I settled comfortably into my seat, trying to conjure up the look of a man with important business. "Do you have a copy of today's *Wall Street Journal*?" I asked the flight attendant suavely. Within seconds, I was tilted back reading statistics I had absolutely no chance of comprehending.

I don't remember the plane taxiing down the runway or taking off. Thirty minutes into the flight, the gentle prodding of a beautiful flight attendant woke me up. "Mr. Davis, would you like a snack?" she asked sweetly. The comfortable chair had overwhelmed me; I'd fallen asleep reading numbers and data. As I returned to consciousness, I was horrified to discover I'd slobbered all over myself as I slept.

"No thank you," I sputtered, "but could you bring me a mop and some super-absorbent paper towels?" Mr. First-Class Featured Speaker at Prestigious Events had spent the last thirty minutes drooling like an idiot. I avoided eye contact with the beautiful lady as she handed me the quicker-picker-upper.

After a lot of dabbing, I looked stained but presentable. The attendant came back my way. I handed her the towel. This action toppled the tomato juice into my lap.

Fortune magazine, *Wall Street Journal*, and all the other trappings of first class scattered as I leaped from my first-class seat. In twenty years of flying coach, I'd never spilled anything. Now, on my first chance to be a big shot, I had the look of someone who'd been lounging in a dumpster. The first-class lavatory was full, so I had to walk all the way to the back of the plane to clean myself up. As I walked through the economic curtain that segregates the aristocracy from the huddled masses, I felt as if I was coming home. Except the common folk didn't appear to be happy to see me. I realized I must be a sight—a walking drool-stained canvas highlighted by broad strokes of tomato juice. I didn't even deserve coach status. Was it too late to request the baggage compartment?

I still looked a mess as I got off the plane. "Have you been sick?" my host asked, mercifully leaving off—"all over yourself?"

"No, I've been stupid," I mumbled as I filed my first-class literature in the wastebasket. "I'll tell you all about it on the way to the hotel. Can I sit in the back?"

Since my tomato juice bath, I've accumulated enough frequent-flyer miles to ride first class many times. I always try to remember that my seating assignment doesn't determine my value. Neither does my home address, my college degree, or my salary. It isn't the books I read or the clothing I wear that gives me worth. I'm a creation of the architect of the universe. I am fearfully and wonderfully made. My eternal soul was purchased with the blood of God's Son. That alone makes me first class.

Just a thought:

First class isn't a standard of living; it's a way of life. I only remember one line from the movie *The Lion King*. In that scene, a voice from the clouds guides Simba. The voice booms, "Remember who your father is." Isn't that great! Because of who my Father is, there can never be any room for putting on airs. I must respond with love and kindness to those around me. I must extend the same mercy and grace that was extended to me. I must realize that God loves me just the way I am—a drooling, bumbling first-class idiot. Loving people with the kind of love with which God loves me—that's the real first class.

The brother in humble circumstances ought to take pride in his high position.   —James 1:9

Wake Up and Live!

I hate my alarm clock. If this isn't an appliance straight from hell, it was surely manufactured in the same zip code.

Sure, I know how innocent and benign some of them can appear. Don't be deceived; they're all the more diabolical for it. When I was a child, a huge alarm clock grinned at me from my nightstand. Large, colorful numbers circled a deceptively gentle face. Perched atop its sweet countenance were two monster ears disguised as bells—and between those ears was a hammer.

When released, that hammer would beat the ears into shrill, clanging submission. I think most residents of our county awoke to my alarm each morning. No complaints; farmers miles away figured it saved them money. Remember roosters? This is the contraption that drove roosters out of business. Like many of us, the once-proud fowl was replaced by a machine. Dependable, hardworking roosters, with years of seniority—displaced by alarm clocks.

The alarm clock tears us from peaceful slumber, just as a shark tears a baby seal from the surface of a tranquil sea. I believe awakening should be a kinder, more Christian process. There should be a stoplight posted at the corner of Asleep and Awake. That way we could approach the intersection slowly, look both ways, and then proceed to Awake. And don't forget, a gentler process would also allow the option of making a U-turn back to the Land of Nod.

But no—alarm clocks force a collision every time. Who doesn't savor that zone of sluggish uselessness before we fully awaken? Why start the day with a terrified leap and flailing arms that might just injure those you love? I ask you, who enjoys starting the day by randomly pounding every item on the nightstand while lunging to slap the ears off that big, round face? Why wake up with your highest blood pressure reading of the day? If your heart rate is 190 when you wake up, what can you look forward to for the next twenty-four hours?

The floppy-eared, goofy-face alarm clocks, like the roosters, have been replaced. In the great evolutionary march of predawn terrorism, we are living in the Age of the Electric Alarm. Yes, they're sleek and modern, but they're sneakier and just as evil. They have a cold, calculating look about them and cold, calculating strategies to match. The alarm is just as loud and offensive; but it contains an insidious new feature that robs you of more sleep than ever.

Seconds before the alarm goes off, the clock begins emitting a soft, buzzing noise. It might be described as a pre-alarm alarm—a prelude to terror. It only serves to rouse you into a state of semiconscious confusion just before it releases its demonic, bloodcurdling screech. Over a period of time, your body learns to prepare for the onslaught of the real alarm when the pre-alarm buzz begins. Videos taken of sleeping people show that at the pre-alarm buzz, the body slowly arches back into an unnatural, almost alien position. The right hand gropes for something to throw. The left hand indiscriminately flops around in the vicinity of the nightstand, searching for a wonderful, nonexistent button to stop the alarm from ever going off.

The left hand is doomed to failure. The wife or husband who is unfortunate enough to sleep through the pre-alarm is often beaten senseless in the melee. During the pre-alarm buzz, the brain begins formulating words that would never be spoken in a fully conscious state. These are words that will come forth the second the real alarm goes off.

The alarm companies tried to soften the impact of their invention by adding a "snooze" feature. It's of no value. It doesn't provide fifteen minutes of extra sleep; it provides fifteen minutes of cringing anticipation of the alarm. You might as well come out from under those covers and surrender yourself.

Actually, alarm clocks are the result of the Fall. In the beginning, Adam and Eve had no reason for alarm. They only became alarmed after the apple-cider incident. Sleepy people need alarms, for we develop destructive habits. We adapt behaviors that threaten our most important relationships. We slowly move away from the God who loves us. Only an alarm can jolt us back to reality.

Some of your friends can testify that an illness, a financial crisis, a close call with death, or a personal loss has shaken them from a complacent sleep. Crisis shook the mist from their eyes and awakened them to the real values in life. Our life-alarms are seldom pleasant but often necessary. We need sleep in order to live, but we cannot truly live while sleeping.

I'm envious of people who don't seem to need alarms. They don't know much about Jay Leno or Nightline, but they know a lot about life. They see sunrises, get exercise, and find time to talk with God. They live their lives wide-awake. If we could only keep our eyes open; if we could be alert in our relationships with special people and with our Lord; if we could rest when rest was appropriate, and live vigorously under the shining sun—maybe then we would need no alarms.

I have more to say about all this, but I hear a buzz . . .

So then, let us not be like others, who are asleep, but let us be alert and self-controlled. For those who sleep, sleep at night, and those who get drunk, get drunk at night. But since we belong to the day, let us be self-controlled, putting on faith and love as a breastplate, and the hope of salvation as a helmet. For God did not appoint us to suffer wrath but to receive salvation through our Lord Jesus Christ. He died for us so that, whether we are awake or asleep, we may live together with him.   —1 *Thessalonians 5:6–10*

The Proof Is in the Tapioca Pudding

I have always been mystified by prayer.

I know it's the process of talking to God. I know he hears and answers. Yet sometimes it seems to me as if AT&T is handling the connection and most of their lines are down. And sometimes it feels that way for extended periods.

Those are the times when I become discouraged. I wish I could know what God is up to. How is he processing the last batch of prayers that went up? We pray for the sick, and they die; we pray for power against temptation, and we fail. When these things occur, the doubts creep in. Can we really believe that God is hearing and caring and responding?

In the midst of those dry days, God does something wonderful: He lets us see a visible answer. His reassurance breaks through like cooling rain. We simply accept that we can't always see his hand or comprehend his ways—but he does indeed answer prayer.

A pastor friend of mine, Joel Morgan, planned on visiting missionaries in Eastern Europe. He asked friends who'd traveled in that area what he should pack. There were many helpful suggestions, but everyone agreed he should bring extra food. While staying in rural villages with no electricity or running water, they might be forced to go without meals. It would be wise to have easily packed snacks on hand for survival rations.

One missionary warned Joel to bring more than he'd need; some of his supplies might be confiscated by customs. Joel asked himself questions as he wandered through a grocery store: *What should I take that won't catch the eye of the customs agents? What will not spoil? What will serve as an energy boost?*

He also whispered this prayer: *Lord, you know the things I'll need and the things that will make it through customs. I'm just going to walk down these aisles, trusting you to prompt me to select the right items.*

Instantly his eyes fell on a display of Reese's Peanut Butter Cups. He put a king-size pack of them in his cart. Further down the aisle he was drawn to an arrangement of tapioca pudding snack packs. (From my perspective, when anyone is drawn to tapioca pudding it's already a miraculous sign.) Finally he scooped up some small cans of fruit cocktail, some gum, and some hard candy. "Surely," he thought, "these items will tide me over if I get hungry."

On the fourth day of the trip, Joel arrived in Timisoara, Romania. He would spend several days with a couple who had labored for fourteen months there. The family had been sent to Romania by a national missions organization, but for all practical purposes they'd been forgotten.

They faced harsh conditions. Heat and electricity were often turned off for days. Joel and his team were the first English-speaking people the missionaries had seen in six months. The simple opportunity to talk to someone was cause for celebration. And their two teenage daughters were starved for anything American. Joel spent some time chatting and praying with the family. As they were about to leave, he suddenly thought about the survival goodies he'd purchased for himself more than a week before.

He had a nice idea. It was only October, but why not use those snacks to celebrate an early Christmas? Giving away his supplies would mean relying on God for the rest of the trip, but somehow he knew this was exactly what God wanted. He retrieved his backpack with all the goodies securely hidden inside (not even the customs agents had been interested in tapioca pudding). Then he sat down with the family in their living room.

Joel took on the role of Santa Claus and played it to the hilt. He asked the two teenage girls, "If you could have one thing from the U.S., what would it be?"

In unison they sang out, "Candy!"

"What kind?" Joel asked, confident they'd love anything he offered.

The mother chimed in: "The girls love Reese's Peanut Butter Cups," she said, "but they're not available in this part of the world."

With a lump in his throat, Joel reached into his backpack and pulled out the king-size package he'd smuggled into the country. (Customs agents *do* like Reese's Peanut Butter Cups.) The girls jumped up and down joyfully, laughing as they held their new treasure between them. Wiping a tear from his eye, Joel asked their mother, "What item from back home would brighten your day?"

It was a risk. What if she wanted, say, a side of beef? But with one miracle already in the bag, what could go wrong? "I miss fruit," the mother replied a bit sheepishly, "especially citrus." Reaching into Santa's bag, Joel extracted a can of fruit cocktail and a tin of canned mandarin oranges.

Now everyone was laughing and wiping away tears of joy. After a time of celebration and amazement, Joel turned to the father. The backpack was nearly empty, and he considered removing the few items and asking the father to make a selection. Two out of three miracles ain't bad; why press his "luck"? But something deep in Joel's soul shouted, "Go for it!" Before he could argue with God, he heard himself ask, "Gary, what's your favorite dessert?"

This wonderful servant of God smiled and said, "It's something no one else in the world likes—tapioca pudding."

Joel nearly injured himself pulling the pudding from the pack and racing across the room to show him the super–4 snack pack of tapioca pudding that God had prompted him to buy seven days earlier and four thousand miles away.

What followed was praise and worship in its truest form. Nine people were crowded into a tiny living room in Romania, weeping and singing praises to God. That day they gained a new appreciation of Philippians 4:19: "God will meet all your needs according to his glorious riches in Christ Jesus."

These good people had left family and friends and familiar ministry behind. They'd been neglected even by the organization that sent them. God knew they needed encouragement and renewed hope. God answered the prayer of a small-town pastor and used Reese's Peanut Butter Cups, canned fruit, and tapioca pudding to remind them that he hadn't forgotten them. He also gave them a glimpse into the mysterious power of prayer.

Just a thought:

Pray with confidence today, knowing that though your prayer may not work out as you thought it would, it will work out. Joel prayed, thinking of what he needed; God answered by providing what a family needed. In the process, he gave Joel a dose of something he needed far more than a slimy cup of tapioca pudding: Joel saw the hand of God. He was allowed the privilege of being the messenger of a miracle.

Pray with confidence today, knowing that God cares for you just as much as he does for the missionary family in Romania.

Pray with confidence today, knowing that though you may only see occasional glimpses of his hand at work, he's always at work. He hasn't forgotten you.

I write these things to you who believe in the name of the Son of God so that you may know that you have eternal life. This is the confidence we have in approaching God: that if we ask anything according to his will, he hears us. And if we know that he hears us—whatever we ask—we know that we have what we asked of him.   *—1 John 5:13–15*

Bettin' Fifty Bucks on the Lord's Prayer

John Cassis, one of the nation's finest motivational speakers, told a wonderful story at a meeting of the Million Dollar Round Table. He was one of the inspirational leaders of the Chicago Bears during their glory years, and he often gave short talks to the players on game day.

As John tells it, Mike Ditka was about to deliver a locker room pep talk one day. He looked up and saw defensive tackle William "Refrigerator" Perry. How could he not have seen him? At 338 pounds, The Fridge stood out even in a crowd of pro football players. Ditka gestured to The Fridge. "When I get finished," he said, "I'd like you to close with the Lord's Prayer." And the coach began his talk.

Meanwhile Jim McMahon, the brash and outspoken quarterback, punched John Cassis. "Look at Perry," McMahon whispered. "He doesn't know the Lord's Prayer!"

Sure enough, William "Refrigerator" Perry sat with a look of panic on his face, his head in his hands. He was sweating profusely. "Everybody knows the Lord's Prayer," said Cassis to McMahon in disbelief. After a few minutes of watching the Refrigerator leaking several gallons of sweat, McMahon nudged Cassis again. "I'll bet you fifty bucks Fridge doesn't know the Lord's Prayer," he dared.

As Cassis tells the story, he stops to reflect on the absurdity of it all: "Here we were, sitting in chapel, and betting fifty bucks . . . on the Lord's Prayer!"

When Coach Ditka finished his pep talk, he asked all the men to remove their ball caps. Then he nodded at Perry and bowed his head. It was quiet for a few moments before the Fridge spoke in a shaky voice: "Now I lay me down to sleep, I pray the Lord my soul to keep . . ."

Cassis felt a tap on his shoulder. It was Jim McMahon. "Here's the fifty dollars," he whispered. "I had no idea Perry knew the Lord's Prayer."

I grew up in a world where everyone seemed to know the Lord's Prayer. Simple prayers and Bible stories were part of a rich and varied American heritage. They were cultural touchstones. Schoolteachers taught from the

Bible; prayer was a conventional backdrop to society. Our country was founded on religious freedom. Now we consider public expressions of faith a violation of someone else's religious freedom. The Lord's Prayer is often considered unwelcome here, offensive there, even illegal in some settings.

The result? This generation suffers from a kind of faith illiteracy. Some men and women and children have never uttered a prayer. They don't know the stories of Abraham or Moses or David or even Jesus. But those wonderful stories have never lost their potency; they still hold the secret of hope for the world. Even the child's prayer, "Now I lay me down to sleep," reflects a simple faith that has changed millions of lives.

Just a thought:

It's still legal in this country to read your Bible. I wonder what would happen if, each day for the next thirty days, you started your morning with a thoughtful recitation of the Lord's Prayer. Then—what if you picked four great Bible stories and read one each week?

Consider the stories of Jonah, Joseph, Daniel, or Moses. If you do this you'll be drawn to the wonder of a great God and encouraged by the simple faith of the men and women who trusted him. I betcha fifty bucks you'll find it a rich and intriguing experience.

Just in case you don't know, this is the Lord's Prayer:

Our Father in heaven, hallowed be your name, your kingdom come, your will be done on earth as it is in heaven. Give us today our daily bread. Forgive us our debts, as we also have forgiven our debtors. And lead us not into temptation, but deliver us from the evil one. For yours is the kingdom and the power and the glory forever. Amen.   —Matthew 6:9–13

Amen.

Take It, Stupid!

I nearly dropped the phone. My head was ringing like a cash register in the express lane. The man at the other end of the line wanted me to speak at a corporate convention. Corporate conventions had real money. I needed real money.

Up to this point in my life, I'd done a lot of public speaking. But most of it was in churches. They didn't have real money—they had "love offerings." There's a difference. A "love offering" is a collection of plates laden with quarters and nickels and garnished with an occasional one-dollar bill. Most of the love offerings I'd received were heavy on love and short on offering. On one trip, I traveled three hundred miles and spoke for three nights. As I left for home, a deacon pressed fifty dollars into my hand and told me this was a small token of the church's love for me. The operative word here was "small."

That's it: lots of love, little offering. I was definitely glad they didn't hate me—then I would have owed them.

But now I had a live one on the line—a corporation. Corporations paid up-front cash. My mind was racing. Finances had been thin ever since I set out on my speaking career. I could hope to earn a couple of hundred dollars from this one speech. The man gave me the dates for his meeting. I put him on hold and called Diane into the room to help me check the calendar.

Diane handled all my booking because of my tendency to book three speaking engagements on the same night at opposite ends of the universe. I'd accept an invitation, hang up the phone, and forget all about it within ten or fifteen seconds. More than once the phone rang as I sat watching football. I developed a neurotic fear of the words, "Ken, where are you?" It happened so often, I was afraid to answer the phone. That's when Diane took over.

But now, Diane pointed out a problem. The speaking date, according to the calendar, fell right in the middle of our vacation. But why be inflexible? I tried to get Diane to hear the beautiful cash-register sounds

I was hearing, but she was tone-deaf. "No amount of money is more important than our time together as a family," she stated firmly. I sighed, politely told the man I wasn't available, and hung up the phone.

But this was one very determined man. He kept calling back, trying to entice me to come. Each time he called, I tried to entice Diane. "He wants me really, really bad," I whined. "Maybe three hundred dollars bad." Diane stood firm; family vacation was simply too important. With each call, the tension between Diane and me escalated.

The man called one final time. I'd grown impatient with his persistence, and I decided to make him an offer he had to refuse. I would set a price so outrageous that he'd have to stop calling.

"Your convention date falls right in the middle of my vacation," I said, "I can only come on one condition." My mind scrambled, jingling the coins that were lying there. "If you pay me . . ." I paused and shot for the moon " . . . fifteen hundred dollars." I'd never in my life seen fifteen hundred dollars in one place. But why stop there? "You'd have to fly my family out to be with me," I continued, on a roll. "And you'd have to put us up in a beach house for three days and pay all the expenses. Then I would come." Those were three conditions, not one. But it didn't matter. It felt good to demand the impossible!

His answer was immediate. "That's great!" he said. "We'll do it."

I dropped the phone. Diane walked into the room just as I picked up the phone—and my jaw—from the floor. She knew what was up. I covered the receiver with my hand and tried to smile. "I tried to make him an offer so ridiculous that he had to turn it down," I explained, trying to break it to her slowly. Her face reddened and her brow furrowed as I continued. "I told him I'd come to his event if he was willing to pay me fifteen hundred dollars and all the expenses to fly you and Traci to join me." I paused for effect. "Plus pay the expenses for three days in a beach house. But he said yes! What am I going to do?"

A smile creased her face. "Take it, stupid!" she laughed. Then she turned and left the room. She's flexible. I love her for that.

I wonder how many times we're blinded to blessings God would willingly give—simply because we're afraid to ask. I'm not suggesting you adopt the same materialistic motivation I had. But could there be times to go to God with requests bigger than we think possible?

Not necessarily for money or fame or power, but for the deepest needs of the soul—for peace, healing, confidence, and the joy of a deeper relationship with him.

God is infinitely bigger than any corporate entity. He owns all the corporations. He possesses all the emotional and spiritual strength that we need, and he freely offers it to us. I know it's not always simple. I haven't always received everything I've asked for—but that should never stop us from asking.

There's overwhelming evidence that God delights in giving us things. He gives wonderful love offerings. Have you asked? You have nothing to lose. In whatever language may be appropriate for the Creator of the universe, he might just respond, "I love you. Take it, stupid!"

This is the confidence we have in approaching God: that if we ask anything according to his will, he hears us. And if we know that he hears us—whatever we ask—we know that we have what we asked of him.

—1 John 5:14–15

I Wanna Sing!

By the time we got to Florida, my nerves were raw. This was no love-offering speaking engagement—this was a $1,500-honorarium, airfare-for-two, three-days-in-a-beach-condo speaking engagement. I felt compelled to come through with a better show than I'd ever produced. I had always done my best, love offerings or not. Where was I going to find the extra *oomph* for this one?

On the evening of the speech, I faced one of the unruliest groups of my career. My speech followed Happy Hour, and several people in the room were very "happy." To make matters worse, the man who had originally invited me didn't show up. Standing in for him was an inebriated stranger who introduced me. "I don't know who our speaker is tonight," he said, "but I want everyone to sit down, shut up, and listen to him." Then he turned and continued a loud conversation with the women standing next to him.

Terrified, I stood to speak. Before I'd finished the first sentence, a nightmare began to unfold. My two-year-old daughter, Traci, sitting with Diane in the back, broke loose and came lurching up the aisle with that Frankenstein walk only children and monsters can do. "Daddy, Daddy!" she drooled as she staggered forward, a huge toothless grin on her face. To be honest, she looked a lot like some of the men sitting in that room.

I tried to stop her with one of those lethal parent-frowns. She ignored the look and kept on coming. Flushed with embarrassment, I spoke. "Traci, go back to your mother," I said, trying to be stern enough so that Traci would get my message and gentle enough not to turn my audience against me.

Immediately someone in the audience shouted, "Let the kid up there! We want to see the kid!"

By this time Traci had reached the platform. I picked her up and, smiling ear to ear, did my best ventriloquist act. Whispering through clenched teeth, I ordered her to say hello, then return to her mother. But kids instinctively sense the power they can wield in a crowd. She grabbed the mike and shouted, "I wanna sing!"

Few things in life are more difficult than trying to discipline a child in front of a "happy" audience. Before I could say a word, another voice from the audience shouted: "Let the kid sing! We want to hear the kid sing!" I hadn't delivered the first sentence of my fifteen-hundred-dollar speech, and already I'd lost control. I longed for a love offering.

Leaning out from my arms, both hands strangling the microphone, Traci began to sing the only song she knew. "Jesus loves me, this I know," she sang, "for the Bible tells me so!" Her eyes were dancing with delight. By the time she reached the second verse, she was in full form. Throwing her head back for the chorus she wailed the finale: "*Yeeeeeeeessss*, Jesus loves MEEEE! The Bible tells me sooooooo!"

The room exploded in thunderous applause as Traci took her bow and headed contentedly back to her mother. She was satisfied. She'd turned a corporate motivational event into a Sunday school class. She could go home now.

As I began my speech, there was a noticeable difference in the room. I saw several people wiping tears from their eyes. The whole atmosphere had been changed by a child's simple musical declaration of faith. Those men and women listened with interest and respect as I delivered my address.

After the program many of them came to me one at a time. There were no questions about business. They came to talk about Traci's song. We exchanged memories of youth and family and church and faith until the early hours of morning. They'd been moved by the shameless enthusiasm of a child singing words of faith. They spoke of happier times than the "Happy" Hours that now punctuated their lives. I wondered if they secretly longed for a childlike courage to replace the bland spirituality now guiding their politically correct lives.

I resolved that day never again to allow my fee or the status of my audience to influence the value I placed on a speech. I also resolved to try to be more like Traci—to exhibit a more spontaneous and natural enthusiasm for a simple yet profound truth: Jesus loves me!

In our efforts to avoid being childish, have we sacrificed the beautiful quality of being childlike in terms of trust and faith and courage?

Jesus said, "I tell you the truth, anyone who will not receive the kingdom of God like a little child will never enter it." And he took the children in his arms, put his hands on them and blessed them. —Mark 10:15–16

Best Friends

Bill Letourneau was a big man. When he laughed, his entire body took part in the celebration.

It all started with his eyes. The Letourneau smile would push those big, rosy cheeks up so far that his eyes would sparkle from little slits. Then he'd begin to tremble with a "tsk-tsk" kind of laugh that sounded like air escaping from a turning Michelin tire. The laughter would escalate, spreading rapidly from lips to shoulders and finally to belly. His cheeks would turn a sunset pink, and the original "tsk" emerged as a rich, full-bodied Maxwell House laugh.

Bill's laughter could fill any two rooms—and it was marvelously contagious. People would come from other rooms and occasionally from other buildings to see what all the commotion was about. We'd often forget why we were laughing. We'd find ourselves laughing at each other laughing.

Bill never met a restaurant he didn't like, but he liked the good ones better. He would check into cheap hotels to save money so he could afford to eat in five-star restaurants. He had a love affair with fine cuisine. His passion for food never went to his head, but it did make its way to the rest of his body.

Weight wasn't an issue with Bill—it was a fact of life. He wasn't what you'd call fat. He looked like a big, healthy football player. On two occasions we competed to see who could lose the most weight over a three-month period. There was one rule: The loser had to treat the sleek, trim winner to a meal at a fine restaurant. What a way to end a diet! Bill gleefully lost the contest both times.

After his first defeat, he and his wife Julie took my wife Diane and me to The Fort, a wonderful historic restaurant just west of Denver. Diane and I arrived early at the authentic adobe fort. When Bill and Julie arrived, he was dressed in a smart, dark suit with a power tie. Hanging from his neck with baling twine was a rough cardboard sign with the following crude, felt-tip inscription: "I have no self-control."

Our laughter was the delightful hors d'oeuvre to an unforgettable evening. Three years later I was once again approaching sumo-wrestler dimensions, while Bill was back in his familiar big-teddy-bear class. It was time for another contest, and once again I endured starvation in anticipation of a free dinner with Bill and Julie. Bill was thrilled to lose again, and I looked forward to another evening of delectable food and sidesplitting laughter. I could hardly wait to see Bill fulfill his part of the bargain. This time he'd promised to wear a sandwich board reading, "I *still* have no self-control."

On April 8, 1998, I was awakened by the angry buzz of our phone. My associate Dan Marlow tearfully conveyed the sad news that my friend Bill Letourneau had died of a heart attack during a mission to aid children in Vietnam.

It took days for the full impact of the loss to hit me. As I prepared a tribute for his memorial service, I realized character qualities in my friend that I'd never previously considered. Not many people know that I'm sometimes uncomfortable in small, intimate settings, but I always loved being in Bill's presence. He put me at ease. I loved his sense of humor. I loved his tender heart. I loved his passion for life. But only on somber reflection did I discover what I loved most about Bill Letourneau.

At fifty-two years of age, I feel safe and in control on the stage or behind a podium, but I still tremble when I first meet people one-on-one. Bill had a wonderful gift that melted that fear. Whenever I met him, whether he was with others or working in his cramped little editing room, when I walked through the door Bill would jump to his feet as though he'd waited all day for this moment with me. Even in large gatherings, he'd spot me across the room and his face would brighten. He'd begin to laugh as he rumbled toward me, teddy-bear arms extended. I felt like the star of any occasion. He made it seem as if the party had been incomplete until I arrived; as if I was the bright spot in his day.

This was the impression of Bill I shared at his memorial service. It must have touched a chord, for several people approached me afterward. Fighting the tears, they told how Bill had made them feel precisely the same way. To be completely honest, this brought me down a peg or two at first. I'd felt this was a thing exclusively between Bill and me. I wanted to be special.

But then I realized the truth: Bill greeted and treated all people with that same enthusiasm. Everyone was the bright spot in his day.

What a gift! I want to be like that. I spend so much time being anxious about others' opinions of me that I often miss the opportunity to express my joy at being with *you*.

I want to make people feel as if the party can't start without them. That's the way God loves—every child is his favorite child.

Thank you, Bill, for treating me that way.

Thank you, God, for loving me that way.

Help me to love and treat people that way.

You Can't Get There by Standing Here

Over the centuries, theologians have argued about the true identity of the "unforgivable sin" mentioned in the New Testament (see Matthew 12:31). I've identified that sin. It is suggesting to a person who flies 150,000 miles a year that travel is glamorous. I get that a lot. When people tell me how fortunate I am to be able to travel, I have to fight the impulse to hurt them.

Those people will not be in heaven. They'll be condemned to eternity in the middle seat of an airliner, sandwiched between a screaming child and a retired sumo wrestler. The seat will be in the very rear of the airplane, next to the lavatory. Their flight will circle in bad weather, waiting for a clearance to land that will never come.

I don't mean to sound vindictive—it's just that I hate travel. There's nothing glamorous about it. If they ever invent those "Beam me up, Scotty" gizmos they use on *Star Trek*, I'll be the first customer.

Starships notwithstanding, there's a profound truth to be found here: Wherever you choose to go, you must travel to get there. As a child I loved going to church, but rarely was the short ride to God's house a pleasant experience. Animosity would build up between my sisters and me during the week. It would explode in the backseat of the car on the way to church. We'd be at each other's throats before the car left the driveway, discreetly punching, kicking, and pinching each other.

The covert jabs, pinches, and hoarse whispers would soon erupt into a brawl that would make Wrestlemania look like a Sunday school class. My dad would grab the rearview mirror and adjust it so we could only see his eyes and deeply furrowed brow. "Do you want me to come back there?" he'd bellow.

"Sure, Dad, you're going down the highway doing seventy-five miles an hour. Come on back—let's see what happens!" I'd cleverly respond internally. I was too young to die, so I never said it out loud.

Sometimes, in an attempt to reach us, Dad would swing his arm over the backseat. We knew the exact length of his arm, and we'd retreat to that one corner of the backseat he couldn't reach. From there we'd continue the battle by mouthing silent insults, searching for the one that would trigger another all-out war.

When I tell this story in public, I'm inundated with parents who identify with it. One parent even gave me wonderful advice on how to coax my children out of that unreachable safety zone: "A tap on the brakes brings them right into play," he confided.

I loved church, but the process of getting there was bone-jarring. I love speaking all over the world, but the journey can be exhausting. Travel is neither fun nor glamorous. Nor is the journey of everyday life particularly exotic. And that brings up a sad truth about many people and the potential they never reach.

Some folks dream of worthy destinations, but they're unwilling to set out on the long journey to get there. They want to experience the thrill of victory without the agony of the feet.

Going to church is liberating . . . but you must endure the ride.

Speaking to several thousand people is exhilarating . . . but you must squeeze into a torturous airplane seat.

A marriage "till death do us part" is beautiful . . . but you must walk through the valley of the shadow of death to get there.

Standing on top of the mountain is a glorious experience . . . but you'll have to swim rivers, wade through swamps, and climb cliffs that block you from your goal.

Too many people die without realizing their dreams because they're unwilling to act on them. Every dream should come with a warning label: "You can't get there by standing here."

Just a thought:

The short, unspectacular step you take today will bring you one step closer to your dream tomorrow.

A Dozen Wilted Roses

I was just collapsing into my easy chair after a long day of work. The chair welcomed me into its arms. I could feel the day's tension drain from my body. That's when Diane made her announcement: "I have tickets for the high-school play."

As far as I was concerned, she could have been waving a coupon for a discount root canal. Spend my evening seeing amateurs stumble through some Broadway musical? Not likely. "I'm not going anywhere," I growled.

Diane persisted. "Jean has a part in the play—we *have* to go!"

Jean was a vivacious teenager who attended our Campus Life club meetings. She was there for the games and discussion, definitely not what she called "religious emphasis." Yet Jean was curious about the person of Jesus, and she occasionally asked some probing questions. Still, she saw me as some kind of religious fanatic.

Diane pleaded as if Jean wouldn't make it through the night without our attendance at the play. I could see I was going to have to put my foot down. "I'm exhausted and we're not going!" I rumbled with intimidating finality. "Jean has only two lines. She wouldn't even know we were there." That was my verdict; the ruling was final.

On the way to the play, Diane saw a man standing on the street corner selling flowers. "Stop!" she shouted, almost causing an accident. "Let's get some roses for Jean!"

"I'm not stopping," I insisted. "We're late for the play—do you want to lose more time? Besides, buying roses on the street is a bad idea. We don't know where those roses have been. And look at the guy selling them: We don't know where he's been either." I presented my argument with overpowering, unassailable logic, then glanced at Diane to see her reaction.

We drove around the block and purchased a dozen half-wilted street roses wrapped in dingy waxed paper. As we drove away, I wondered where the *paper* had been.

The play was one of the worst I'd ever seen. Scenery toppled over, actors walked to the wings to get their lines, and at one point the curtain came down prematurely. Unskilled voices reached for unattainable notes and missed by just enough to send shivers through the entire audience. I could see the hairs stand up on the neck of the person in front of me as voices scraped the scale like fingernails on a blackboard. I was miserable. The roses, too, were visibly suffering through the performance. Talking to flowers supposedly invigorates them, but this was killing them.

The final curtain came none too soon. I tried to make a run for the door, but Diane clamped down on my arm. "We have to give the roses to Jean," she whispered threateningly.

"Who wants roses that have been tortured to death?" I mumbled as we headed backstage.

If you haven't already guessed, Diane is the real minister in our family. She's always thinking of others. All I could think about that evening were my own needs. I was focused on me, and I was miserable. I was tired. I was bored. I had wanted to stay home. But attending the play wasn't about me. It was about Jean.

I learned another thing as we waded through the backstage throngs of screaming teens. The most ineptly performed, musically excruciating play is an Academy Award performance to the kids in the cast. Diane and I were watching all these teenagers bursting with excitement. Suddenly there was Jean. When she spotted us, she ran squealing down the hallway. "What did you think?" she bubbled.

"You were marvelous," Diane gushed. "You stole the entire play with your entrance." Jean looked to me; it was my turn to gush. But my gusher had been killed by the A-flat in the last scene. I quickly thought of the dead flowers.

"Here, these are for you," I spurted—kind of a "mini-gush." I pushed the sweaty waxed paper-wrapped bundle toward her. Wide-eyed, she grasped the flowers. She stumbled back against the wall, then slid down until she was sitting on the floor.

Her voice caught as a tear trailed mascara down her cheek. "Thank you for coming," she said in a trembling voice. "I only had two lines. I didn't think you'd come." The sweet smile on Diane's face perfectly camouflaged the I-told-you-so kick that jolted my shin. Out onstage, the leading lady was still gathering dozens of beautiful roses (from legitimate florists) thrown by the audience. I doubt all those roses together moved her the way a dozen wilted, musically abused roses did Jean.

Monday afternoon there was a knock on my office door. It opened just enough for an eye to peer through the crack. "Can I come in?"

asked the eye. Jean swept into the room, pulled up a chair, and straddled it backward with her chin resting on the chair's back.

After some small talk about the play, she came right to the point. "Tell me about Jesus one more time," she asked. So once again I talked about the sacrifice he'd made. I explained the forgiveness he offers to all who trust him. When I finished she said, "I'm ready." Before I could give any counsel she closed her eyes, her chin still resting on the chair, and she prayed one of the simplest and loveliest prayers of commitment I've ever heard.

When I opened my eyes she was looking directly at me. Without a sound her lips formed the words *thank you*—and then she was gone.

The years that followed confirmed the fact that what happened in my office that day was real. Another truth was also confirmed. Jean's final step of faith had little to do with the dozens of successful Campus Life meetings I'd led. It was all about a dozen cheap roses, a wad of sweaty waxed paper, and a horrendous high-school play. Ministry comes down to love focused intensely in a single direction. I was a messenger; my wife was a minister.

Just a thought:

I'm glad God is more like Diane than me. He gave up the glory of heaven to come to our play. (And a bad play it was.) He brought only one rose. (And a beautiful rose it was.) That rose was crumpled and ruined by a sin-mangled song that was once the beautiful melody of heaven. Because of that rose, I came to God and said, "I'm ready!"

Thank you, God, for coming to my play. Make me more willing to bring roses to someone else today.

And If I Die Before I Wake

Parenting isn't for weaklings. Moms and dads must be stout of heart; they find that out quickly.

But there's one task that strikes fear and desperation into the toughest of them. You know the one: trying to enforce bedtime. Children have a deep, instinctive aversion to sleep. They'll climb any mountain, cross any river, swim any ocean to avoid closing their eyes.

Our youngest daughter Taryn devised the strategy of calling out religious questions from the bedroom. It's the old Pharisee maneuver. One night, the fleeting tranquility of bedtime was broken by her inquiring mind's need to know. "Daddy, does God talk to us?" she shouted with Socratic intensity.

"Yes, God talks to us," I responded sagely. "Go to sleep. We'll discuss it in the morning." Being a fool, I imagined that would satisfy her.

"No, we must discuss it now!" she yelled back. "God just spoke to me!" Before I could frame an appropriate theological response, she added, "He said I could get up!"

How do you deal with that? Here's a child who doesn't know the meaning of the word *psychology* and she's already deftly placed me in the palm of her hand, psyched out.

One night, the bedtime battle reached epic proportions. It was a battle waged with weapons of quick wit and childish charm. In other words, I didn't stand a chance. I'd been struggling for thirty minutes, trying to get my other daughter, Traci, to settle down. Finally I put my foot down.

"Go to bed!" I commanded.

"I need a drink of water," Traci shot back without hesitation.

The verbal sparring match intensified. "You can't have water."

"Why?"

"You'll wet the bed."

"I've quit."

(How do they respond so quickly? Do they have a game plan? Do they pull random thoughts out of thin air? Is this the root of original sin? But I wasn't whipped yet.)

"You didn't quit wetting the bed," I countered. "You wet the bed just last night."

She was quick. "The cat did that!" She said it without hesitation, without blinking. Maybe she was going to be a lawyer.

I ignored the opportunity to laugh and embrace the teachable moment. Instead, I made my move to protect my authority. "Don't tell me the cat did it!" I bellowed. "The spot on your bed was the size of a large pizza! We only have a tiny little kitty."

"It wasn't our cat," she replied without missing a beat. She was a true professional; she was the best. Yes, she was going to be a lawyer.

And she was shocked—*shocked*—that I wouldn't believe her. I held her by the shoulders. "Look me in the eye," I insisted, "and tell me the truth."

Her bottom lip began to quiver; a huge, martyr's tear welled up in her eye. "I'm sorry, Daddy," she sobbed. "But a big, giant cat took the screen off my window and jumped on my bed. He wet on my bed, and then he jumped back out the window." Sensing my skepticism, she continued. "He put the screen back on after he left; that's why it's still on now." I was speechless.

"He was a big cat!" she appended during my gaping silence.

I was coming to a slow boil. "I can't believe you'd lie to me like this," I scolded. "I want you to go straight to bed and I don't want to hear a peep out of you." (I learned that one from my father. Evidently such sayings lose their power between generations; I could hear her in her bedroom making tiny little peeping sounds.)

Then, after a few more moments of precious, lovely silence, a defiant little voice screeched from the bedroom. "Daddy, I want water and I want it now!"

The gauntlet had been thrown down! My parental authority was up for grabs. I had only one option—I called on the sacred and hallowed words of parents across the reaches of time. "If I hear one more word from you," I roared, "I'll come in there and give you a spanking!"

"When you come," she sang out sweetly, "bring a glass of water."

I let out a great sigh, knowing when I was beaten. If *I* could think that quickly, I'd be a millionaire. "Go get your water," I laughed, "and then you get to bed or I'll come in there!"

But she wasn't done with me yet—not this night, not Traci. About twenty minutes later I realized I hadn't heard the pitter-patter of her little feet returning to bed. "Traci, what *are* you doing?" I called.

"Drinking water," she replied.

"No one can drink water for twenty minutes," I grumbled as I stomped to the bathroom. I was wrong; children trying to avoid bedtime can basically do anything. These are the signs and wonders the Bible talks about in the Last Times. I opened the door and gazed upon a child who'd been quietly sipping water for twenty minutes. Her little belly looked like a basketball.

"You get to bed right this moment!" I barked.

This, of course, signaled a new phase in the negotiations. I closed my eyes and waited for the words I knew would come. They came. "I have to go to the bathroom."

Of course I had to let her go or the giant cat would be back.

She still wasn't done with me. The next time I looked up, she was standing in the hallway, stark naked. She had her hands on her hips and that "whatcha gonna do about *this?*" look in her eye. Before I could respond, she took off. "Catch me!" she giggled as she zipped past me. I bolted out of my chair and bounded in clumsy pursuit, forgetting that God has equipped his naked children with the ability to turn on a dime.

She sprinted into the kitchen and hung a sharp right. I was wearing wool socks. On a linoleum floor with wool socks there is no such thing as a "sharp right." I lost control, spun out, and totaled my wife's new blender.

I walked away from the crash, a bit shaken up, removing shards of glass from my body. Then to my horror I saw my naked daughter dash out the front door. What had started out as a power struggle between a parent and a child had now escalated into a neighborhood incident. This is how world wars begin. My daughter was running naked down the street, shattering the quiet of twilight as she sang, "Catch me! Catch me!"

I caught her about a block away from home. Then I remembered I was wearing only the moth-eaten woolen socks and a pair of old underwear.

I scooped up my giggling Godiva and ran the fastest hundred-yard dash of my life. Once back in the safety of our house, I laughed until it hurt.

I dared to inquire one day: Whence cometh this dread of bed? "Monsters and prayers," said my daughter without looking up from her toys.

Monsters I understood. On more than one occasion I'd conspicuously sprayed "monster repellent" (water in an old Windex bottle) in the closet and under the bed to assure a safe night. But prayers? What could they possibly have to do with fear of the night?

The explanation forced me quickly out of the room. I needed to laugh without hurting her feelings. The child's prayer that begins "Now I lay me down to sleep" had been less than helpful during her formative years. One phrase in the prayer had imbedded itself in her mind: "If I should die before I wake . . ." All the antics were to avoid that twilight zone where monsters live and people die.

Just a thought:

There's something about the night that can be frightening, even for adults. Many a night I've tossed and turned, my heart racing, as I worried about a monster problem that had to be faced the next day. Some of those dark nights of the soul were spent contemplating my own mortality or fretting over my family's safety and security. Some were spent agonizing over damaged relationships. Not really much different from a child's fears, are they?

Yet somehow the morning light cuts those night-monsters down to size. They don't go away—but they don't seem quite so monstrous anymore. The morning brings hope.

There are also hours of eclipse, when the darkness hangs over us even in the daylight. Monster spray is useless in such times. Only the brightest light can disperse the lingering shadows of despair. Only the Lord's face can shine through and provide us with strength for today and with bright hope for tomorrow.

You are my lamp, O LORD; the LORD turns my darkness into light.
—2 Samuel 22:29

One last thought: Turn on the light!

Getting Taken for a Ride

It happened at a traffic light near the edge of town. A man gunned the engine of his huge Harley Davidson motorcycle as he waited for the light to change.

You might have been tempted to stare at this fellow—and he would have enjoyed it. A filthy rag was fastened around his head. From beneath it a matted tangle of oily gray hair spilled down the back of his tattered leather jacket. Images of skulls and bones leered from his clothing and his bare forearms, and his bike bore the emblem of a menacing black widow spider. As he waited at the light, an elderly man in a lime-green moped pulled up beside him. The ringy-ding-ding of the moped was drowned out by the roaring thunder of the Harley.

"Boy, that's some motorcycle you've got there," the old man croaked. "Mind if I take a closer look?" Scowling from behind his oily beard, the biker gave him the once-over. "If that turns your crank, old-timer," he snarled, "go ahead and take a gander."

The old man was a little farsighted, but he wanted to take in all the scenery. So he leaned his face right over the bike and examined every inch. Looking up after a while, the old man grinned and said to the biker, "I bet that motor-sickle goes fast!"

But no sooner were the words out of his mouth than the light changed. The biker thought he would show this old geezer what a real chopper could do. He gave it full throttle and within thirty seconds, the speedometer read 199 MPH. He chuckled with satisfaction.

But suddenly he noticed a dot in his rearview mirror—a dot that was growing larger. Something was gaining on him! What could it be? He slowed a little to get a better look, and whatever the thing was, it flashed past him so fast he couldn't even identify it. The thing disappeared over the horizon, whipped around, and came right back at him. As it zipped past, he recognized the rider. It was the old man on the lime-green moped! How could this be?

The biker took another look into his rearview mirror. There was that speck again, coming back his way and growing larger! The biker tried to outrun it, but it just couldn't be done. It was a moot point within seconds, for the moped slammed into the rear of the Harley Davidson. The collision destroyed both bikes. You could hear the impact for miles.

The biker extricated himself from the mangled steel pretzel that had once been his beloved Harley Davidson. But the old man had fared even worse. He lay groaning beneath the blackened, smoking remnants of his moped. Even the hardened biker was moved with compassion. He knelt beside the old man's face and softly asked, "Is there anything I can do for you?"

The old man choked, coughed, and replied, "Yes. Could you please unhook my suspenders from your handlebars?"

This story came to me over the Internet. When I read it, the punch line caught me so utterly off guard that my uncontrolled laughter disrupted the office. People came running over to see if I was all right. Several times during the day, I thought of that story and began laughing all over again. The visual images alone were sufficient to double me up.

I later told the biker tale to an associate of mine. This friend has a wonderful, dry sense of humor, but he rarely laughs out loud at anything. The greatest response I've ever received from him was a smile and the proclamation, "That's extremely humorous." This time he grinned after the punch line and said, "I guess you have to be careful where you hook your suspenders."

That was his dry wit speaking, but it was also his wisdom. It started me thinking. I know the story is no more than a joke and, as such, can only be stretched so far metaphorically. But there is a lesson here.

You and I wouldn't purposely hook our suspenders to anything dangerous. And yet many of us might be willing to lean over for a closer look. And that's what is so insidious about sin. It looks so good to us. It catches the eye. The thunder of its engine seems to hold the promise of high adventure and intense thrills our moped could never provide. It may never be our intention to get on and take a ride. But let us just get a little closer—can't hurt to look, right? Let us feel the power. Let us smell the leather. What harm could come?

The world around us is littered with the mangled lives of men and women who never intended to get hooked. They only wanted a closer look at the shiny colors of some forbidden sin. There's the husband who never intended to lose his family, but decided it was okay to flirt along the boundaries of adultery; now he pulls himself from the smoking wreckage of his marriage.

There's the teenager who never intended to seriously use drugs but saw no harm in experimenting; now his life is twisted and disfigured by addiction.

There's the woman who was willing to skim a small sum each year from her company—how could just a few dollars be wrong?—because she was tired of driving an old Ford when all her friends were in BMWs. She never intended to end up in jail.

Or how about that man whose moral restraints finally gave way as a result of that first "harmless" peak—only a quick glimpse—at the glossy pornographic images available on the Internet. "How far does this go?" he wondered. In the months that followed, like the man on the moped, he never saw the light change. Before he knew it, he was dragged faster and further than he ever thought possible.

Just a thought:

Here's a fairly intense—but life-saving—thought for today:

Sin never fulfills its promises. It will take you farther than you wanted to go, keep you longer than you wanted to stay, and make you pay more than you could ever afford. Be careful where you hook your suspenders.

Be self-controlled and alert. Your enemy the devil prowls around like a roaring lion looking for someone to devour. Resist him, standing firm in the faith, because you know that your brothers throughout the world are undergoing the same kind of sufferings. —1 Peter 5:8–9

The Brass Monkey Principle

Have you ever said the following during a prayer? "I'm never going to do *that* again!"

Many of us say it regularly—about the very same *that*. All we do is change the emphasis. I'm never going to do *that* again. I'm never going to do that *again*. I'm *never* going to do that again.

Eventually we grow discouraged and become resigned to doing *that* for the rest of our lives.

The problem is that we focus on the problem rather than on the solution. *That* becomes our master. And we make ourselves prisoners of the very things we yearn to avoid. A college speaker once taught me the lesson indelibly. "Tonight, when you go to bed," he said, "I'm asking you not to think of a brass monkey. When you pull the covers back, you may think of anything you'd like—but don't think of a brass monkey. And all day, whenever you think about going to bed, remind yourself not to think of a brass monkey."

That night, when I pulled back the covers of my bed, brass monkeys were frolicking on my nightstand, perched on my lamp, and screeching and chattering beneath my pillow. They were everywhere, inescapable. Throughout the day I had thought about nothing but brass monkeys.

I harbor a few brass monkeys in my life. Let me tell you about one of them.

I travel over a hundred thousand miles a year. I hold frequent-flyer status on two separate airlines. Some people believe travel is glamorous and exciting. I'd like them to know it's frustrating beyond belief. I now have luggage in major cities all over the world. They ought to hang mistletoe at each baggage check-in location—because as soon as they take possession of your stuff, you can kiss it good-bye. The next time I go to the airport, I'm going to set a bag down and tell the handlers, "Take that one to Burma, this one to Anchorage, Alaska, and this piece can go with me to Denver."

The boy behind the counter will say, "We can't do that."

Then I'm going to say, "You did it yesterday!"

I'm not very proud that travel mishaps often ignite within me a less-than-gracious spirit. Translation: I can get really mean and nasty. Each of my last three flights has been delayed over two hours. I've missed connections and meetings, and I've been late getting home. On such occasions I often become ... uh ... unpleasant. Yet before I leave I look in the mirror, lift my right hand, and say, "I won't allow myself to lose my temper. I will treat people with respect." Translation: I will not see a brass monkey.

When I get into these predicaments, I don't get all hot and bothered and start calling everyone names. That would be too easy. Instead, I employ devious, covert tactics to make them uncomfortable.

I know all too well that the people with whom I square off tend not to be the perpetrators of the problems. They simply have the sad job description of dealing with people whose lives are disrupted by such malfunctions.

One night I arrived very late and very weary at a hotel where I held a guaranteed reservation. I was informed at the desk that my room had been sold to someone else. There was no room in the inn. The brass monkey reared his ugly head. Rolling my eyes like an adolescent, I began grunting and groaning about the meaning of the word *guarantee*.

"What does the word *guarantee* mean?" I asked the poor girl behind the desk. "In your dictionary, does it say that *guarantee* means 'we'll keep your room until someone else asks for it'?" Danny, my traveling companion who has a cooler disposition, saw the foam building up at the corners of my mouth. Danny stepped forward, put a hand on my shoulder, and gently offered to handle the problem. His sane approach resulted in us being upgraded, at no additional cost, to a suite of rooms so big it took in two time zones. We had half the entire floor. There was room in the inn after all.

Even as we made our way to the new, palatial set of rooms, I was still grumbling about how someone could sell our guaranteed room. By the time we reached the fifty-sixth floor where the suite was located, I felt like a total fool. In spite of my prayers and preparation to avoid the curse of the brass monkey, the first bump in the road turned me into a spoiled child.

When Diane first started playing golf, she demonstrated a peculiar gift. Her golf balls seemed to be water-seeking missiles. If there was water anywhere on the golf course, her ball would find it. One day, after baptizing six balls, we came to a fairway without a drop of water in sight.

Diane teed up with confidence and hit her best drive of the day. We watched as it soared gracefully through the air and landed—with a splash!

A quick review of the scorecard confirmed it again: no water on this hole. Puzzled, we started toward Diane's ball. Reaching its landing spot, we dropped our bags and started laughing. It just so happened there was a six-inch indentation in the middle of the fairway for the sprinkler system. There, sitting at the bottom of this itsy-bitsy pool of water, was Diane's ball. Even golf balls abide by the Brass Monkey Principle.

Just a thought:

Rather than concentrating on the behavior we would avoid, why not concentrate on the behavior we desire and the God who can make it possible? If you're constantly thinking of the negative things you're trying to avoid, you're going to be obsessed by those things. Even children know that the Little Engine That Could chanted, "I think I can, I think I can." He didn't chug up the hill puffing, "I hope I don't, I hope I don't!"

A biblical fellow named Paul complained that he always ended up doing the wrong things instead of the right ones (see Romans 7:19). He nailed it—the solution—right on the head when he wrote:

Finally, brothers, whatever is true, whatever is noble, whatever is right, whatever is pure, whatever is lovely, whatever is admirable—if anything is excellent or praiseworthy—think about such things. Whatever you have learned or received or heard from me, or seen in me—put it into practice. And the God of peace will be with you. —Philippians 4:8–9

Getting in Character

I have this compulsion: I need to be in control. At airports I stand and watch closely until my luggage disappears into the bowels of the luggage world. I need to be sure no one forgets to put it on the belt. Then I sprint for my window seat so I can peer out to be certain my bag is being loaded on the plane.

When I ask my secretary to do something, I double-check and triple-check just to be sure she doesn't forget. I get to meetings early so I can control the lighting and make sure the seating is appropriate. Then, when something goes wrong during the meeting, I'm on my feet seeking out the right people and the right solutions.

In my own eyes I feel that I'm in control, but it's all an illusion. I know how I appear to others—as stressed-out as a mother hen taking her brood on a field trip to a weasel farm. When I got married, I quickly learned there was one thing I couldn't control. When our children were born, I found out there were *several* things I couldn't control.

I managed to control my kids to some small degree until they reached the age of accountability (around eighteen minutes after birth). Then my control was limited to the superficial behavior they exhibited in my presence. Once they were out of sight, it was another form of control that took over: their character. Character is the factor that ultimately calls the shots in our everyday lives.

The true mark of character is not visible to the human eye. Character is defined by what we do when no one's looking, when we believe there's no chance of getting caught. Our public behavior is little more than a reflection of what we'd like others to think of our character.

I once lived a dual life. The life I lived at home and at church was inconsistent with the private life I lived on the road. I managed this lifestyle by rationalizing my behavior. I wasn't as bad as many people I'd observed. I didn't go in for any of the really serious stuff—at least that's what I told myself. In truth, I was on a fast track to destruction.

I was not a promise keeper; I was a promise breaker. I was living in a spiritual vacuum, and I knew it.

I came to a point where I couldn't go on living a life in violation of the principles I knew to be right. Sickened by my own behavior, I finally sought counseling. My heart was broken over the details of my daily life.

But I had yet to experience true brokenness. With painful honesty I poured myself out to the counselor, who guided me back to spiritual and moral health. As I was cataloguing my sins in what I felt to be a cleansing act, he halted me abruptly. His words hit me like a blow to the stomach.

"This isn't a matter of bad deeds," he said. "It's a matter of bad character."

I could handle admitting my individual sins. What I couldn't do was come to grips with the fact that I was sinful at the core of my being. I wanted to fall back on the line used by comedian Flip Wilson and say, "The devil made me do it."

The devil hadn't made me do anything. Each time I made a bad choice, it was *my* choice. I could have chosen to do the right thing, but my choices sprung from the condition of my character—a character grown stagnant from lack of challenge and spiritual growth.

One doesn't change character by changing behavior—it's simply not that easy. Such efforts bring short-term results. What I needed was a change of heart. That transformation did come to pass, and it was the most painful and the most liberating one of my life. I knew I'd missed the mark of excellence and purity that God intended for me. I stood exposed and vulnerable before a holy God to acknowledge the darkness of my own heart.

I knew I deserved the uncompromising discipline set apart for sinners such as me. Yet in that moment God did just the opposite: He gave me the best. Forgiveness, love, and acceptance flooded over my parched soul. Joy and sorrow mingled together in a bittersweet way; joy for the grace being extended to me, and sorrow that I'd lived so badly in the face of such love.

Theologians tell me this is the act called repentance. My friends and family tell me it has had a profound effect on my character. All I know is that I must respond to such love with a life that honors the One who poured it out on me. I no longer place such a high value on being in control. I want the One who cared for me in the darkest hours of my life to shape my character and my life.

The greatest word in the Bible is the one found in Romans 6:23. It is the word *but*. Listen to this:

When you were slaves to sin, you were free from the control of righteousness. What benefit did you reap at that time from the things you are now ashamed of? Those things result in death! BUT now that you have been set free from sin and have become slaves to God, the benefit you reap leads to holiness, and the result is eternal life. For the wages of sin is death, BUT the gift of God is eternal life in Christ Jesus our Lord.
—*Romans 6:20-23, emphasis added*

If there were a period after the word *death*, there'd be no life or hope for our character. But there's a comma followed by the word *but*—and what follows makes all the difference in the world. It provides the power and motivation for building character in my life. "*But* the gift of God is eternal life in Christ Jesus our Lord." There is hope for all of us.

Get on Your Trike and Ride

Being the father of two girls isn't an easy role in our society. The toughest part comes when boys begin taking an interest in your daughters. Handling that crisis demands wisdom and discernment.

I remember the first boy who walked brazenly up to my door and asked if Traci could come over to his house. I told him my daughter wasn't that kind of girl. "You have a lot of nerve," I said. "I don't want to see you hanging around here anymore." He took it quite well, got on his red tricycle, and rode away.

Because I remembered my own teen years when my adolescent hormones outnumbered the brain cells in my body, I projected my distrust on any male child who could walk. If the male in question had a car, the distrust increased tenfold. If he owned a van, I sought to keep him outside the city limits.

Several years after the tricycle incident, I was helping Diane clear the table when another young man darkened my threshold. I watched through the window as he approached the house and chickened out twice. It could have been he was afraid of my daughter, or it could have been my reputation had gotten around. Whatever the case, he was trying to work up the courage to ring the bell. As he approached the third time, I tiptoed to the door and slowly turned the knob. When I heard the boy step up to the doorbell, I yanked the door open and thundered, "WHAT DO YOU WANT?"

The boy leaped back, his eyes as big and shiny as compact discs. I realized I was still holding a large butcher knife in each hand. I'll give him credit for this much—he approached again. "Can Traci come out, or can I come in?" he stammered.

"Do you now own, or did you ever own, a red tricycle?" I growled, rubbing the edges of the two knives together. Before he could answer, I tapped one of the knives on the screen door. "You look a lot like the kid that killed my parents." He backed away several steps. "I'm just kidding," I said with a high-pitched cackle. "I killed my own parents— come on in!"

He did. But I'm sure the word spread about the Davis girls' dad. Many of the boys who came over later would stand some distance from the door and shout with cracking voices, "Is anybody home?" Some never got out of their car.

I wasn't as fierce as I've led you to believe, but I did worry about the spiritual and physical welfare of my children. Later in life I learned to teach by example and open communication, rather than by guilt and intimidation.

I had to learn to trust God with their lives. My heavy-handed rule was influential only to the extent of my reach. Ultimately, it would take God's hand of love to keep them on the straight and narrow. I wish I'd been more proactive in talking with my daughters about the issues they'd face in life; and I wish I'd been more deliberate about pointing them to faith in God. My blustering bombast required much less courage—and it wasn't very effective. It certainly didn't stop the boys from coming. I'm so thankful that both girls chose to marry men who loved them and also loved the God who created them.

Recently my youngest daughter, beautifully dressed in white, stood beside me at the back of the church. Standing at the front of the church was the young man who was about to become her husband. I couldn't have done a better job if I'd picked him myself. Yet despite his strong character and wonderful reputation, I was still the father. As much as I'd grown to love him, I still looked at him as the pervert who stole my little baby girl. But I wasn't the one in control here. I was never really the one in control. As we stood waiting for the ceremony to begin, she squeezed my arm and whispered, "I love you."

I found out later that she didn't say it because she loved me (even though she surely does). She and her sister had made a bet that they could make me cry during the ceremony.

I didn't cry. It did throw me off though. When the pastor asked, "Who giveth this woman to this man?" I answered, "My mother and I do."

After a wonderful reception, they left on their honeymoon. The four-wheel-drive vehicle they took to the mountains was packed with gifts, camping equipment, and clothing. As they drove away, I thought I saw—packed in the very back, beneath a backpack—a red tricycle.

God loved your children so much that he sacrificed his Son for them. Lighten up. He can be trusted.

The Three Greatest Words on the Face of the Earth

What could be better?" I asked myself smugly, leaning back in a comfortable lounge chair on one of the country's most beautiful beaches.

Spread out before me was the Gulf of Mexico. Sitting beside me was opportunity personified: a man who wanted me to appear in one of his films. No, it wasn't a big-budget action thriller, it was an industrial training film. But that didn't matter to me—this was my big chance for the silver screen; that first big step to stardom. I gazed at the gripping script of our blockbuster. I was oblivious to the fact that my daughter Taryn had slipped away from her mother and was wading in a sewage lagoon.

With a gorgeous beach at her disposal, Taryn had chosen to play in a little green pond with a very big smell. Later she explained that she chose the sewage treatment lagoon over the beach because she liked the colors better.

As I dreamed of stardom, Taryn was draping reeking algae all over her body. When she'd completely cloaked herself in the stringy goop, she came looking for me. She peeked up over a sand dune and saw me deep in discussion with the filmmaker. Here came my precious daughter, galloping toward me, bathed in fumes with the potential to clear the beach.

I didn't see or hear her coming. She hit me doing at least thirty miles per hour. At impact, the clammy slime unwrapped from her little body and wrapped itself around me. I tried to leap upward, but her cold, smelly arms were clamped around my neck. The angle of the chair gave her the leverage to keep me down. She grabbed me by the hair, yanked my head around, looked deep into my eyes, and proclaimed, "I love you, I love you, I love you! I kill you with love, because I am the *loooove monster!*"

Then she proceeded to "kill" me with sloppy, odorous kisses. Appalled and disgusted, the movie guy leaped to his feet and frantically brushed bits of algae from his fancy shirt. "Could you please ask her to leave until our business is finished?" he sniffed.

Dripping with goo and still in the grip of the love monster, I responded. "Sir," I said, "our business is finished now." I had no desire to do business with someone who could remain unmoved by the words of a smelly, slime-covered child proclaiming, "I love you, I love you, I love you!"

I don't know when the words "I love you" were first spoken to me. My first memory of the words comes from a girlfriend who spoke them without knowing what they meant. Still, the words sounded so wonderful. Just writing about it brings back some of the emotion.

The words "I love you" shrink the universe to one moment in time. In that moment nothing else matters, no one else exists. "I love you" gives meaning to life. When people find themselves in life-threatening situations, the words "I love you" are often the last words spoken. They are the words we most want to hear. The sound of my wife Diane saying those three words is like beautiful music to me.

Then why are they often so difficult to say?

I love to hear my grown children say, "I love you." When they were small, they spoke the words freely. They'd leap out from behind a sofa in ambush, giggling with delight at my reaction. Then they'd gleefully indulge in the spontaneous hugs and kisses that always accompanied those three words. After being put to bed, they'd yell, "I love you," because they knew those words would buy ten more seconds of "awake." I didn't care about their motives; I loved to hear the words.

When my oldest daughter Traci was fourteen, she stopped saying the words. I tried to coerce her. I'd force eye contact and say, "I love you," conspicuously waiting for a response.

"Me too," she'd intone without emotion.

"Then say it," I would demand.

"I just *did*," she would respond, incredulous that I couldn't see that "Me too" was equivalent to "I love you." But it wasn't the same.

Years passed. She turned sixteen, then seventeen. When she was eighteen years old, I stood in a tiny college-dorm room at John Brown University. I held her close for a moment and spoke the words one more time. I held her by the shoulders, looked into her eyes, and said, "I love you."

My heart broke when she said, "Me too."

On the way home I fought waves of grief and sadness. I wondered what I'd done to deserve this cold response from someone I loved so much. It made no difference that something in her life might be making it difficult for her to express her love. I simply wanted to hear the words.

Several months later I was invited to speak in a chapel service at her school. I felt nervous as I delivered my message. I didn't want to embarrass my daughter. I stumbled through my message. Afterward, the chaplain invited me to join him for lunch at a quaint Italian restaurant. We'd just begun to eat when he reached into his briefcase and pulled out a stack of blue response cards used by the students to critique chapel programs. He told me he'd never seen such a positive response from the student body. Then he went on to read several very positive comments from the cards.

As I took another bite of spaghetti, he pulled a single blue card from his coat pocket and said, "Here's a card I think will interest you." I laid my fork down and took the card. Neatly printed on the front was my daughter's name—Traci Lynn Davis. I stopped chewing. On the back of the card was a space where the students could write their critiques and comments. What if she didn't like my talk?

Summoning courage, I flipped the card over. Written on the other side were these words: "I love my daddy!"

I spit spaghetti all over the table. I excused myself and stumbled to the bathroom, locking the door behind me. Hot tears spilled out. "Oh, thank you, God!" I wailed. "She loves me! She loves me!"

How could I have known there was someone else in there? From one of the stalls, a disgusted voice growled, "Get a life, man!"

Five years have passed since that spectacular spaghetti-spewing day. Traci is now married and lives a few miles from our home. As I write this, I'm returning from Jacksonville, Florida, where I performed for six thousand people. The positive response of the audience was tremendous. The previous day I had had two successful presentations in Gatlinburg, Tennessee. Just this morning I received the news that one of the top talent agencies in the country is interested in my work. But those events weren't the highlight of my week.

When I was packing the car to leave on this trip, Traci, who now works in our office, came out and smothered me with a big hug and said those three precious words: *"I love you."*

When my wife Diane left me at the airport, she kissed me softly and said, *"I love you."*

When my youngest daughter was leaving after her wedding on Saturday, driving away to start a new life with her husband, her last words were *"I love you."*

As I read from the Bible this week, I was reminded that God knows all the darkest corners of my life. He knows my selfishness, my fear, and my cowardice. He's aware of all the times I've miserably failed. Yet he sacrificed his Son for me. With that act, God shouted, "I love you!" with more affection and meaning than mere words could have ever conveyed.

It was a good week filled with good news, but those words—"I love you"—were the highlight of my week. "I love you" is the best news of all!

A Story Worth Telling

I was never comfortable giving my Christian testimony as a young man. I thought I wasn't eligible. As I saw it, only two kinds of people were qualified testimony-givers:

1 Famous overachievers
2. Terrible sinners

The overachievers tended to be athletes who'd caught the winning touchdown pass in the last ten seconds of the game. They testified how they couldn't have done it without God. My greatest athletic achievement was getting through an entire day without hurting myself. I have the hand-eye coordination of a carp—a fish with lips.

The sinners were those new believers who'd been saved from lives of debauchery. I lacked the right stuff there too. My first memory is that of playing the part of Joseph in a Christmas pageant. Whenever the church doors opened, I was in the building: Sunday morning worship, Sunday night fellowship, Tuesday night Bible study, Wednesday night youth group, special prayer meetings, and the obligatory Christmas pageant Joseph practice—I was there for all of it.

What testimony could I possibly give? I didn't smoke. The fire of alcohol had never touched my lips, and (much to my chagrin) no one else's lips had ever touched my lips. I listened to the horrible sins and huge successes of the testimony-givers, and wished I, too, could have a real, prime-time testimony.

I had two options: I had to start some serious sinning, or I'd have to make something up. I dreamed of standing before an awestruck audience, my voice trembling with emotion: "I killed twenty-five people with a wet squirrel," I'd confess, warming them up for the really good stuff. "I was into drugs. I shot peanut butter directly into my veins. It was crunchy peanut butter—it drove me nuts."

After a pause for effect, I'd continue, "I had a quart of liquor every day and a different woman every night." I could picture the older people, heads shaking and tongues clucking in disapproval. I could see the youth leaning forward in their seats, waiting for the details. It was time to deliver the punch. "Then, when I was four years old, I accepted the Lord; and I've lived happily ever after ever since."

That story would surely be more powerful than the truth, which would go like this:

"Folks, my life of sin began the night I stole a cookie as my parents slept. I cheated on a test, and once I looked at a picture of a naked woman in National Geographic Magazine. [That was the only image of nakedness I'd ever seen—until I was fourteen, I thought all naked people had bones in their noses.] Then I met Jesus. Today, I'm still tempted and I still face many trials in my life."

What kind of testimony is that? Who'd be encouraged to follow Jesus by hearing such a proclamation?

Maybe people who are honest would want to hear that testimony. Maybe there are folks looking for a God who forgives and who continues to work in the midst of their imperfections. Maybe people like that would listen to testimonies from people like me.

Yes, God has miraculously intervened in the lives of flamboyant sinners. I'm not belittling those miracles. But even in those testimonies, I believe a strong dose of reality is essential.

Those dramatically saved from their wickedness face daily struggles too. Even when the big-league sin is left behind, the garden-variety sin is there to be faced.

Besides, we should recognize that God doesn't categorize sin. The miracle of a nice little church boy experiencing forgiveness means as much to God as the conversion of the drug pusher down the street. And I should also recognize that I wasn't always the nice little church boy. As my Christian pilgrimage unfolded, I managed to get some "legitimate" sins under my belt. By the time I reached forty, I had rug burns from backsliding.

Those dark times taught me a valuable lesson. I've listened to hundreds of people tell how they were lost in sin and sadness, then accepted Jesus Christ—and since then, life has been heaven on earth. All their problems have gone away. I've learned that when struggling Christians hear these words, a sense of hopeless failure settles over their lives like a wet blanket.

Your problems don't go away after conversion at all. Actually, becoming a Christian brings a whole new set of them. Old friends may mock your commitment. You're faced with moral decisions about things you once did without even thinking. I became friends with some of the "happily ever after" people, and only then did I realize they had as many problems as I did. But their real lives didn't match their surreal testimonies.

Christianity never promises an escape from life's trials and temptations. Rather, it's a place to find the courage and faith to withstand them. There's a big difference: One outlook makes empty promises of a storm-free life; the other offers true shelter in the time of storm.

None of the disciples embellished their testimonies with touchdowns. These were average guys who repeatedly failed to live up to the standard Jesus set before them. But they found forgiveness and strength in the face of every trial. And they were willing to die for what they believed. I think they'd have trouble listening to testimonies that say, "Once I found Jesus, my troubles were gone."

Even the godly and upright apostle Paul admitted he was on a journey. His life ambition wasn't to tell people what he'd done in the name of God—it was to shout to the world what God had done for him. His greatest testimony wasn't the absence of struggle, but his enduring faith in the midst of it.

Just a thought:

Be encouraged. No matter what your background may be, you and I both qualify to shout to the world, "In spite of my weakness, he still loves me!" And the greatest testimony is this: to persevere at the business of trusting him daily for the strength we need to press toward the mark of being everything he created us to be.

In this world you will have trouble. But take heart! I have overcome the world. —John 16:33

No News Is Bad News

It was 1985. I was flying in cold, gray clouds at seven thousand feet, and I knew I was in trouble. An inch of deadly ice protruded from the leading edge of my plane's wings. Such ice had killed many pilots in the past, but I thought I could manage it. I began to climb.

Suddenly there was the smell of something burning—and white, acrid smoke flooded into the cockpit and stung my eyes. I knew my situation was critical. There's nothing more dangerous for a pilot than an in-flight fire. Combined with the ice that was accumulating on my wings and my inability to see the ground, the odds against survival were formidable.

With no time to waste, I radioed for help and received a quick response. The flight controllers knew that my situation was critical. The fire had forced me to shut off the electrical instruments I desperately needed to fly in the clouds. Without them, I was flying blind in an airplane quickly turning into a Popsicle. I had only one hope for survival: my communication link with the controllers. I had to keep them apprised of my situation, and they had to keep me informed as to where I might be able to land.

Poor weather conditions had shut down most of the airports within striking distance. Minneapolis was one option. It had radar to guide me down—and fire equipment in case the landing was unsuccessful. By the time I reached Minneapolis, there'd be no fuel left for a second try. It was a life-and-death situation. But I felt confident that working together, the controllers and I could find a way out of this mess.

That sense of assurance was quickly shaken. In order to give me proper radar coverage, the controller asked me to change to a different radio frequency. He told me I'd be talking to people who would guide me all the way down to the runway. He encouraged me to stay calm, he wished me luck, and he gave me the new frequency. I quickly tuned it in and asked for help.

Dead silence.

Five minutes seemed like five years as I called for help. Without guidance, I was facing certain death. I lacked the fuel to get to clear weather, and fire had destroyed the instrumentation I needed to land in the poor weather. Only communication with the controller could save my life. I switched back to the old frequency.

No response.

Now I was terrified. I tried other frequencies, hoping I might run into one that would get me through. In my panic, I forgot the frequency I'd originally been assigned. As I frantically twisted the dial, my earphones were suddenly filled with the sweetest sound in all the earth: someone calling the numbers of my plane.

The controller carefully guided my plane through the fog to a tense but safe landing at Minneapolis International Airport. If communication hadn't been restored that day, chances are great I would have become a sad statistic of what happens when people don't talk.

Just a thought:

When you are receiving no news, that's bad news. Relationships without communication are destined to crash.

Sometimes people find ice on the wings of their relationships. They smell the smoke of disaster. But they retreat in silence from the painful work of confrontation and reconciliation. When pilots respond to an emergency in this way, they die. I'm alive today because I kept trying.

Talk to your spouse. Talk to your children. Talk to your friends. Talk to God.

No Pain, No Gain

"How did they find me?" I thought as I stared at the letter. "How did they know?"

Since I'd hit forty-eight, the AARP had been harassing me to join the ranks of the elderly. Together we'd have the power to march hand in hand—toothless, gray, and aching—demanding the legislation necessary for us to enjoy the golden years of life.

There are distinct pros and cons to getting older. Let me deal with the bad news first. I'm certain you've heard sayings like, "Use it or lose it" and "No pain, no gain." I've developed a new slogan for the mature soldiers of our generation:

"If you use it, it's going to hurt."

During one of my father's visits to my home, we were taking a drive. We passed a batting cage. No matter how old you are, you never lose the need to impress your father. I'd never been in a batting cage, but in my youth-ministry days I'd played lots of softball. This would be a great opportunity to watch my father's eyes light up as he saw my fluid swing and heard the crack of the bat.

The line for the professional fast-pitch machine (ninety-plus MPH) required a half-hour wait. I didn't know this would turn out to be a blessing from God—I only knew the other machine's sixty-MPH softies would present me no problem at all. I positioned my dad where he'd have a great view of me crushing these grapefruit, and I dropped four quarters into the machine. Four quarters buys the right to swing at twelve balls.

I wasn't even in the hitting stance when the first ball whizzed by. No fair! A bit red in the face, I swung hard at the second pitch, which had passed by a while back and was on its way back to the machine. I looked back at my dad. Mercifully, he seemed distracted by someone knocking the covers off the pitches coming from the ninety-plus machine. "I'll get the hang of it in the next few pitches," I thought. The crack of my bat would bring his attention back to the real hero, his own flesh and blood.

Twelve balls came and went. My bat touched nothing but air. I was grateful the bat was still in my hand, because now I could lean on it while I dug in my pocket for more quarters. I took my shirt off—not a pretty sight for an overweight, out-of-shape geriatric. The guy in the fast-pitch cage must have gotten a glimpse of my body, because he missed the next two pitches.

I put four more quarters in the slot and whiffed twelve more balls. I even held the bat out, hoping a ball would just hit it. I could always say it was a bunt.

After four dollars and forty-eight pitches, I hadn't even nicked one. Humor gives an author a little license for exaggeration; this is no exaggeration. I didn't touch one ball with that bat. Soaked in sweat and humiliation, I could only pray that my dad was impressed with my determination.

I asked him if he'd like to try it. Perhaps he'd respect me a little more if he could see how incredibly difficult it was. He just smiled and shook his head. Being in the ranks of the old for a while is much better than when you've just enrolled. He was too wise to swing at a baseball to prove a point, only to pay the price of immobility for the next three months.

After about an hour of play, the score was Machine 48, Ken 0. No runs, no hits, and one big error: When I saw the machine, I should have kept on driving.

Dad and I talked for hours that evening, and I was getting sleepy. The first sign I'd made an error came as I excused myself and tried to rise from the sofa to go to bed. I began to flounder like a turtle turned on its back. The sofa was just deep enough so my stiffening body couldn't extract itself from its grasp. What if I died here? My family (after several minutes of laughter at my expense) pulled me from the Venus sofa trap, and I shuffled off to bed.

The second sign I'd made a critical error came the next morning. I can deal with stiffness, but I'm no match for pain. I sleep in a waterbed. I should have slept on the sofa. It took a SWAT team to extract me from that sloshing prison. I struggled to the bathroom and prayed I wouldn't have to call for help to get out of there. I stepped into the shower. I couldn't wash my hair. I couldn't even raise my arms above my shoulders. How can you be certain you have a head if you can't touch it? At least the mirror offered confirmation that my head was still there, even if I hadn't been using it.

By that evening, I could once again touch my head—though with great pain. After another twenty-four hours, it was a matter of some deep muscular pain. And after a week, all that remained was a deep, abiding commitment never to do such a dumb thing again.

This all happened several years ago. Just the other day I drove past another batting cage. Without fear I parked my car, walked over to the cage, and reached into my pocket. I put a five-dollar bill in the change machine—and put all five dollars worth of quarters into the hand of a child who was gazing longingly into the minor-league sixty-MPH cage.

It felt good to know I'd just purchased a half hour of frustration for the lad. On the way back to my car, I heard the bat crack. Then again. And again.

I didn't look back. I just drove away in disgust.

Unfortunately, the careful avoidance of pain, discomfort, or even inconvenience goes far beyond the batting cage. The prevailing philosophy today seems to be "If it feels good, do it. If it doesn't feel good, avoid it like the plague." The whole philosophy was summed up on a T-shirt I saw. As a parody of the "No pain, no gain" motto, it said, "No pain! No pain!" Message? Avoid pain at all costs.

Regardless of your age, the plain truth is this: If you use it, it's going to hurt. The right way out isn't always the easy way out.

The easy way out of a struggling marriage is to walk away. The more difficult choice is to pay the price to make it work. That's going to hurt.

The easy way out in the face of temptation is to give in. The more difficult choice is to endure an awful longing and do what's right. That hurts.

The easy way out in choosing between sacrificing for others or taking for ourselves is to close our hearts and look out for number one. The more difficult choice is to be selfless with our time, money, and personal opportunity. And that always hurts.

The right decision often involves inconvenience, sacrifice, and pain. Yet the end result makes it worth the price. Weightlifters endure pain for the reward of bulk and strength. Withstanding temptation may leave a desire unfulfilled, but it results in a gain of character and strength that must be bought with a price. And we always get what we pay for.

I hope I never grow as flabby and weak in character and spiritual maturity as I am in the batting cage. Reach into your pocket, take out a quarter, and determine that today, when God makes you aware of a choice you must make, you'll make an effort to do the right thing. You'll be stiff and sore for a while, but eventually you'll be stronger in character and spirit.

Swing away!

The Truth About Cats and Dogs

A dog looks at you and thinks, "You feed me, you pet me, you give me shelter, and you love me. You must be God." A cat looks at you and thinks, "You feed me, you pet me, you give me shelter, and you love me. I must be God."
—*Anonymous*

The doctor's words were kind and soothing as Diane and I wept at the passing of our friend. He'd taken his last breath just moments before, and already I missed him deeply. On the way home we were reminded that only hours before he'd sat between us, soaking up the love we offered and trying to be brave in the midst of great pain.

Now Schultz, our beloved friend of fourteen years, was gone. Why did we grieve so bitterly over the loss of a dog? We tried to convince ourselves it was silly. But there was no denying the genuine sorrow we felt.

Diane and I are not alone. Most homes have at least one furry resident whom they love as a full-fledged family member. Why do we adore these animals—especially dogs—so much?

My guess: It's because they love to live, they love to love, and they love to be loved. We have a new puppy now. We named him Cohiba— Cobi for short. A *cohiba* is a big cigar. My neighbor named all her dogs biblical names like Deuteronomy and Jesse. She gave me a very odd look when I told her our dog was named after a cigar. But our dog looks like a cigar and smells like an ashtray, so Cobi it is.

When we first got Cobi, he was terribly frightened of the stairs. When we were upstairs, he'd sit at the bottom whining until someone carried him up. When we were downstairs, he'd wail until someone would carry him down. Yesterday I lay down beside him and helped him go up the stairs one stair at a time. Several times I had to lift his little rear up to the next step.

After we made it to the top, I carried him back down and set him at the foot of the stairs. A blur of fur, he raced up the steps and yipped at me: He wanted me to carry him down again. So once more, I lay beside him and this time carefully helped him down the steps one at a time.

That day he wore himself down to a fuzzy lump, practicing his newly discovered skill. He must have gone up and down the stairs fifty times. He loves life. Dogs are that way; that's why we love them.

It doesn't matter whether you're gone for five minutes or five days. When you return home, your dog greets you as if you'd just returned from the grave. He'll be jumping, sniffing, licking, barking, and wagging his whole body.

This is why I'm pretty certain cats aren't Christians. (Okay, I know this is going to get me into trouble.) If you come home after a brief trip to the supermarket, your dog is overwhelmed with joy. But your cat will be sitting in your chair hissing, "You left it, you lost it."

I know this upsets cat owners. After speaking on this subject, I got a three-page letter from an irate woman proclaiming that her cat certainly was a Christian. She enclosed a picture of her kitty watching Christian television programming. She insisted he'd leave the room when MTV came on. Later she sent another picture of her cat praying—final proof that he was a Christian. I'm not saying cats are bad and can't be lovable. I just don't think there will be litter boxes in heaven.

When I pet my dog, he goes into a state of ecstasy. He closes his eyes and leans into me with his body. He revels in loving and being loved. Sometimes, just to tease him, I'll stop petting him and not move a muscle. His eyes will fly open, and, in desperation, he'll force his nose up under my hand, then push his body through to get the full petting effect. My hand never moves, but he walks back and forth beneath it; I've become a kind of self-service petting machine.

In contrast, our cat, Pepper, just pretends to love me. She'll snake back and forth around my feet, rubbing against me and making that motor sound that seems so adorable. But as soon as I reach for her she's gone. She's back in my chair hissing, "I was here first."

I caught my cat the other day. I found out she was afraid of the vacuum cleaner, and I cornered her in the bedroom. I didn't hurt her, but she's really clean now. "I'll teach her how to love," I thought. I began petting her rigid, resistant body. When my hand got halfway back, her rear end went way up in the air. Disgusted, I dropped her to the ground. "Gross kitty," I scolded. "That isn't Christian behavior."

Now I want you to relax, especially those of you who are feeling very defensive about your cats. It's a firmly implanted tongue that causes the bulge in my cheek. In spite of the fun, the truth remains. The fact is, we *can* learn a little bit about being lovable from our pets.

What if we greeted each other with the same enthusiasm and joy with which our pets greet us? (Sniffing excluded!) What if we were as quick to forgive and forget? What if we exhibited the joy for life that Cobi exhibits as he bounds up and down the stairs?

What if we were as loyal? What if we reveled in being loved the way they do? What if we loved as enthusiastically? What if, no matter how severely we were wronged, we just kept coming back to love and to be loved. What if?

Just a thought:

In order to keep a true perspective of one's importance, everyone should have a dog that will worship him and a cat that will ignore him.

—*Dereke Bruce*

Who Am I?

What kind of person would you like to be?

If I were to answer that question I'd say, quite sincerely, that I wanted to be kind and patient and well-known for my love for people.

What kind of person does your behavior say you are?

That's a different question. For me, an honest answer would have to include such words as short-tempered, easily offended, and selfish.

Several years ago I boarded a cruise ship in Vancouver, British Columbia. I was scheduled to perform as the ship sailed to Alaska, and I'd shipped several boxes of my books and videos to Juneau a few weeks earlier. The idea was to sell them onboard, which is the source of most of an artist's income on these cruises. But the space is limited on these ocean liners, and the artists are known to jockey for prime spots to display their wares. Watching that spectacle provides a little extra comic entertainment.

We kid each other about the artist competition, but I can imagine how we appear to the passengers—like hyenas scurrying around to mark their territory. When I got on the ship, I found a spot and reserved it by placing a small white tablecloth over that area. I had staked my claim.

Janet Pascal is a wonderful gospel singer with a sweet disposition. She couldn't board with us in Vancouver, but she planned to meet the ship in Juneau. By the time we pulled into Juneau, the good-natured jostling for position had already taken place. There was an unwritten understanding of whose space was where. Up to this point, I'd come out quite well in the territory game. Fully confident that my space was secure, I disembarked to claim my boxes.

Janet was waiting in Juneau, and she had her materials with her. As she boarded the boat she was oblivious to the turf wars.

I must reemphasize that Janet is one of the most gracious and unpresumptuous people I've ever met. She's not pushy or imposing, and she'd never intentionally take advantage of another person. She writes and performs songs revealing a tender and loving heart. But on this day, she made a serious mistake upon boarding the boat. She assumed that the open space with the white tablecloth was unclaimed. She invaded my territory.

Innocently she stacked her tapes and books in the spot I'd so carefully marked and protected. When I—the man who desires to be gracious, loving, and kind—saw that my table was taken, my response was just the opposite of the behavior for which I wanted to be well known. Instantly I was angry and jealous and resentful.

I didn't plan to respond that way; I didn't want to respond that way. But I did respond that way. As I stood grunting stupidly and gesturing in disgust, Janet walked into the room—and I made a conscious decision to act badly. I said nothing about the issue but chose to show my displeasure in a cowardly way. I treated Janet with cool indifference and disrespect. The tone of my voice and the coldness of my greeting let her know I was upset. Even as I did this, I was embarrassed by my behavior. When we got back to the cabin, my children pointed out how rude and childish I'd acted—always a pleasant way to have your misbehavior brought to your attention. They'd seen the hurt and confusion in Janet's face.

How quickly my heart had turned to anger and self-defense. Paul wrote, "The fruit of the Spirit is love, joy, peace, patience, kindness, goodness, faithfulness, gentleness and self-control" (Galatians 5:22–23).

If those were the fruit of the Spirit, from what tree did I fall? The list of my behaviors for the past day had been just the opposite of Paul's list.

Am I a prisoner of my impulsiveness? Is there hope for me? Apparently Paul, too, struggled with this issue. He said, "I do not understand what I do. For what I want to do I do not do, but what I hate I do" (Romans 7:15). Hey! Paul's behavior wasn't perfect, either. He continues:

So I find this law at work: When I want to do good, evil is right there with me. For in my inner being I delight in God's law; but I see another law at work in the members of my body, waging war against the law of my mind and making me a prisoner of the law of sin at work within my members. What a wretched man I am! Who will rescue me from this body of death? Thanks be to God—through Jesus Christ our Lord! —Romans 7:21–25

There is hope. Here's Paul's directive for coping with our selfish, ungracious nature:

Recognize the source of hope.

Those who belong to Christ Jesus have crucified the sinful nature with its passions and desires.   —*Galatians 5:24*

Walk with him.

Since we live by the Spirit, let us keep in step with the Spirit.
                                                —*Galatians 5:25*

Grow up.

Let us not become conceited, provoking and envying each other.
                                                —*Galatians 5:26*

I climbed a mountain in Juneau that day and had a little talk with God. On the way back down I picked a bouquet of wildflowers and had them delivered to Janet's room with a note of apology and a request for forgiveness. She not only acknowledged the apology and forgave me, but she became a dear friend of our family. We often have the privilege of working together. We approach each other with respect: I treat her with loving-kindness and she avoids any table with a white cloth.

Just a thought:

Even though Paul struggled with the same dilemma I faced, he didn't give up. We need not give in to that sinful nature. If I depend on my own desire to be good, I make myself a prisoner of my own nasty nature. It's only through Jesus Christ that I can find the hope of improvement.

God's Wife

There are gushy stories that manipulate the emotions—then there are tales that genuinely pluck the strings of your heart. It's a very fine line between the two.

The following story plays beautiful music on my heartstrings. This one came to me via the Internet. I came within a breath of banishing it to the cyber-trash basket designated for gushy stories, but on further review I decided to salvage it. This is more than just another Good Samaritan tale. It's a challenge to each of us to live up to our heritage as God's children.

It's a cold December day in New York City. A ten-year-old boy stands before a shoe store on Broadway, barefoot and shivering. He peers intently through the plate-glass window. A woman walks up to the boy and asks, "Little fellow, why are you looking into that window so earnestly?"

"I was asking God to give me a pair of shoes," the boy replies.

The lady studies him for a moment, then quietly takes him by the hand. Together they walk into the shoe store. Inside, she asks the clerk to bring a half-dozen pairs of socks for the boy. Then she asks for a basin of water and a towel. He quickly brings these.

The woman takes the little boy to the rear of the store and removes her gloves. Then she kneels, washes his little feet, and dries them gently with the towel as the clerk appears with the socks. The woman places a pair of them on the boy's feet. Then she selects a pair of shoes in his size, bundles the remaining socks, and hands him the package.

She pats him on the head, smiles, and says, "I hope you feel more comfortable now, little fellow."

As she turns to go, the wide-eyed little boy catches her by the hand again. He looks up into her face and asks her, "Are you God's wife?"

How many lives do we touch in such ways that people wonder if we're directly related to God?

What If the Dog Had Been Sitting There?

I will admit it right up front. What you're about to read comes from a male (that's me!) perspective. But in the end, this is really about what it means to be an adult. Please don't judge me harshly for the reckless behavior in this story. I was twenty-two years old—just a child.

The apostle Paul wrote these words in 1 Corinthians 13:11: "When I was a child, I talked like a child, I thought like a child, I reasoned like a child. When I became a man [an adult], I put childish ways behind me."

Paul was thinking of himself when he wrote those words. That leads me to believe either:

1. He was more mature than I am (a very real possibility), or
2. I'm way off on my estimates of the age when adulthood begins (also a very real possibility).

Before I became a man I was taught we arrived at adulthood by way of puberty. At age twenty-one or so, I stumbled through that passage having made little progress in my spiritual or emotional maturity. In fact, I didn't pack away my complete set of "childish things" until well into adulthood.

Childish things often got me into trouble. For example, shortly after Diane and I moved into our first home, a friend gifted me with a box of M–80 firecrackers. Actually, *firecracker* is the wrong word to describe an M–80, which explodes with the force of a quarter stick of dynamite. This happened before they outlawed the stuff.

Adult? A genuine adult wouldn't have been in such a hurry to experiment; he would have waited for some appropriate moment of celebration, like the Fourth of July. Then, taking every conceivable precaution, he'd have ignited his fireworks at a safe distance from any known members of the animal or plant kingdom.

An adult would have received a reality check when three fish floated to the surface after he set off an M–80 in the lake.

But I didn't think like an adult. I thought like a child, and I even invited a fellow adult-size child to join me. We stacked several cement blocks on top of an overturned five-gallon bucket, put one of the M–80s underneath, lit it—and ran.

We were hiding behind the same tree when the M–80 went off. It completely shredded the metal bucket. Twisted shards of metal were embedded in the tree we were crouched behind.

An adult would have fallen to the ground in tearful gratitude for being alive. An adult would have been able to stop laughing as his wife, sprinting from the house in the firm conviction that someone had been shot, inquired when her husband was going to grow up. An adult would have surrendered his remaining artillery rather than allowing his preadolescent mind to race on to other possibilities.

During Diane's ensuing lecture, I did do some thinking. I was thinking, "I wonder how far an M–80 could launch a screwdriver?"

Giggling with infantile glee, my friend and I scampered to my home's unfinished basement. There we produced an old length of pipe. I quickly located a screwdriver that would slip neatly into the pipe. Then I put an M–80 in the bottom of the pipe, and slid the screwdriver down on top of it. Then I lit the M–80 while holding the pipe against the cement basement floor.

By some miracle, I wasn't killed. The explosion knocked me over, left a small crater in the cement floor, and slammed the screwdriver through a one-inch board right up to the tool's handle.

Unfortunately, that one-inch board was the floorboard to the kitchen just above us. There was no mistaking the anger in Diane's voice as she summoned us upstairs. An adult would have been horrified to see the still-vibrating screwdriver blade sticking up through the floor. "Look at that!" Diane thundered. "What if the dog had been sitting there?"

An adult would never have answered, "He'd have moved!"

Later, we were serving our sentence of hard labor in the basement, clearing the debris, when we spotted the old toilet bowl. The previous owner, dreaming of completing the basement someday, had installed a commode. Now moldy and forgotten, it had never been used.

To the childish mind, the mental image of a toilet lid flying open from an M–80 explosion represented the height of hilarity. It was far too uproarious to resist. We lit a stick, threw it in the bowl, flushed the toilet, and ran.

We were huddled behind an old brick chimney when the M–80 did its thing. It quickly became clear that we'd stepped over some forbidden boundary of decorum. I saw porcelain shards hurtling through the dank basement, and I heard the trickle of water. A quick peek revealed fragments of porcelain hanging from battered water pipes that had been transformed into a new, gushing fountain for our basement.

An adult wouldn't have laughed. An adult wouldn't have driven his wife to confiscate the remaining M–80s—to put away his childish things. An adult would have felt some sense of remorse.

An adult wouldn't have had to spend weeks in Time Out to ponder his actions. After twenty-two years of life, I still hadn't grown up. I thought as a child; I reasoned as a child.

My behavior that day soared right off the Foolhardiness Index, even the children's version. But the more outrageous antics soon became a part of my past—partly because I matured and partly because I wanted to stay married.

The child in me hasn't vanished completely. Several years ago I accompanied Diane on a shopping trip to the Mall of America—a very stouthearted and manly deed on my part, if I do say so myself. Shopping tends to be a spectator sport for me, but on this particular day a beautiful jacket seized my attention. With one look at the price tag, Diane declared the jacket beyond the well-guarded borders of our budget.

In a flash of insight, I recalled the proven effectiveness of throwing tantrums. I'd mastered the technique during my career as a six-year-old. Did I still have the knack at forty-five? Was I up to the challenge? There was only one way to find out: I began to pout, "I want the jacket." I wheedled and whined. I stamped my feet.

My family laughed nervously, edging away in embarrassment; they were well acquainted with my capacity for making a scene. As we made our way out of the store and into the mall, I whispered softly to Diane that, unless I got the jacket, I was going to throw a full-blown fit right there in front of hundreds of people.

"You wouldn't dare," she said.

Those were the worst words she could have uttered.

She had just waved a red cape in front of a bull. She had just placed the final straw on the camel's back. She'd laid down a gauntlet I wasn't about to ignore. (Go ahead, play along at home—insert your own cliché here.)

There in the central area of the largest mall in America, before hundreds of healthy retail consumers, a full-grown man fell to the floor and began to rant and cry, kicking and beating his fists on the floor: "I want the jacket! I want the jacket!"

You know what? I got the jacket. I guess Diane never read James Dobson's book *Dare to Discipline*.

The Davis family laughs again and again as we relive that event. At the same time, I can't dismiss the immature, childish urges that plagued my life deep into physical adulthood. Some of them still nibble at my aspirations of maturity. There's nothing funny about those little infantile demons; I find great joy in diminishing their role in my life.

Childish behavior tends to reflect childish thinking. Children, after all, are oblivious to anyone's needs but their own. They entertain no alternative but instant gratification. It shames me to admit how long it took me to see the needs of those around me; how long it took me to comprehend God's wonderful gift to me of my wife and my children; how long it took me to begin satisfying God's will for my life rather than gratifying my own selfish desires.

I'm amazed by how long it took me to put away the childish things— and yes, I'm amazed by how quickly I can pull them out yet again.

Maturity. Adulthood. Manhood. Womanhood. These are not gifts we unwrap at a given birthday party. They must be earned painfully, personally. There are young people who exhibit prodigious maturity, and there are "adults" who ceaselessly function as emotional toddlers.

Jesus loved the spontaneous trust and imagination of children. He loved their capacity to love and to be loved. Those are characteristics to cling to. However, a selfish view of life is a childish view of life. Paul makes that point in the context of discussing selfless love: "When I was a child, I talked like a child, I thought like a child, I reasoned like a child. When I became a man [an adult], I put childish ways behind me" (1 Corinthians 13:11).

The selfish child in me doesn't disappear at some precise moment when I mystically become a man. Rather, it's when the selfish child in me disappears that I have, in fact, become a man. Let's put a new spin on Paul's wording:

When I was a child, I talked like a child, I thought like a child, I reasoned like a child. When I stopped talking like a child, thinking like a child, and reasoning like a child—it was then I became a man.

So when can you and I look forward to full maturity? Perfect manhood? Perfect womanhood? When will the selfish child in us pack his or her bags for good? In Paul's next verse he gives the answer: "Now we see but a poor reflection as in a mirror; then we shall see face to face. Now I know in part; then I shall know fully, even as I am fully known."

When I see the Lord, I'll be complete. Until then, I hope to find increasing maturity—and not to find those M–80s Diane confiscated from me.

Rump Roast

I was heading for the ministry when I finished high school, so my next stop was Bible college. I ended up at Oak Hills, a conservative little Bible school set in the beautiful north country of Minnesota. The school had no academic accreditation in those days, but I received a wonderful education. I left the school fully prepared for ministry and for life.

Today my alma mater is a fully accredited college. It's still theologically conservative, but the place has loosened up considerably since my day. Long gone are the days of prohibiting drums and guitars as instruments unworthy of God. Outmoded rules and regulations for student life have been replaced with sound and sensible codes of conduct. I cherish my experiences at Oak Hills, but the strict regulations and attitudes made for some interesting encounters.

From its inception, Oak Hills emphasized missions. We'd often have chapel services led by missionaries on furlough from exotic locales. One of these guest speakers was an elderly man who'd spent his entire life in mission work. I can't remember his name or where he served, but I'll never forget his message.

After opening with the usual formalities, this man paused and switched to a serious key. He wasn't smiling. "Most Christians," he said, "have moss growing on their butts."

There was a collective, audible gasp from the audience. I am certain the word "butt" had never before been uttered within those walls. One of the deans rose halfway from his metal folding chair—then sat back down.

The speaker continued in his grave tone: "The moss grows on their backsides and on the pews where they sit. It grows because they never move. They've been sitting there for years, crying out, 'God, if you want me to do something for you, if you want me to serve you, then open a door and I will respond.'

"Over the years," he continued, "the moss has grown thick as these people do nothing but sit on their rear ends, waiting for God to open a door." The dean was standing now. The old man's dead-serious tone and the words themselves made it clear he wasn't seeking to be gratuitous—he was making a point, and a wonderful one at that.

It was only as he concluded his message that he allowed a twinkle into his eye. "My life," he testified, "has been filled with excitement and adventure. Paul didn't say he'd sit quietly waiting for God to show him a detailed plan for the future. Instead he said, 'Forgetting those things which are behind, and reaching forth unto those things which are before, I press toward the mark for the prize of the high calling of God in Christ Jesus.'

"If we just sit around waiting for doors to open," he went on, "we'll still be sitting here ten years from now. All my life has been like a ride in a wonderful speedboat." Now his eyes danced with fire. "I've trusted that God was calling me to his service. I've used common sense and prayer as preparation, and I've never slowed down. I've driven my speedboat at full throttle, crying out, 'Lord, if you don't want me in there, shut the door!'"

The old man was grinning as he turned his back to us and exclaimed, "Look! There's no moss growing on my butt!"

I'm sure there were some people who thought this man was crude. Some may have dismissed his choice of illustration as the inappropriate ramblings of a senile mind. But he caught the imagination of many of us in that room.

His mind was not senile. He hadn't lost his bearings, though he described people who have done so. He described folks who refuse to take action. They keep waiting for God to knock them off their pews with the force of a miraculous and supernatural call. This elderly missionary convinced me the call was already in place. Jesus has called all of us to follow him. The next step of faith . . . is to MOVE!!!

Just a thought:

Do a moss check.
Trust God.
Take a chance and move!

Forgetting those things which are behind, and reaching forth unto those things which are before, I press toward the mark for the prize of the high calling of God in Christ Jesus. —Philippians 3:13–14, King James Version

"I've Lost My Father"

Everyone, no matter how hardened or cynical, responds emotionally to the sight of an animal cuddling its young. It touches a chord deep within us that certifies us as feeling human beings. We were created to be touched. On a regular basis we need arms encircling us with encouragement and tender caresses. Our souls are fed by tender words of love, friendship, and caring.

But if love is food, too many people today are starving. It's a problem particularly for men, many of whom have never experienced true intimacy.

In the summer of 1996, I stood perspiring on the platform at Soldiers Field in Chicago. Stretching before me were eighty thousand male, sunburned faces, all gathered for the Chicago Promise Keepers rally. The temperature at midfield was well over a hundred degrees. Ambulances were ferrying to the hospital men who were suffering from heat exhaustion. Stadium personnel with water hoses were firing rainbow-colored fountains of spray to cool the crowd.

And I was speaking. With so much going on all around, these weren't the perfect conditions for captivating an audience. My topic was love. I was challenging fathers and sons to express love to each other.

Jesus didn't express his love through e-mail or fax. He chose to leave comfort and glory just because he loved us. He clothed himself in the fragile body of a human and submitted to a humiliating death. He reached out to those he loved with hands that healed body and soul. He held children and hugged lepers. He professed his love for us over and over, then left us with a record of it so we'd never forget. He prayed for us. And just before he died, he directed us to love each other the same way he'd loved us.

I challenged eighty thousand men to take a simple first step. At the end of my message, I asked them to stand, turn to their sons and fathers, and put their arms around each another. Needless to say, such expressions of love aren't offered cheaply to anyone who walks by. Not everyone has the liberty to touch or hold us close. But what about fathers and sons? Shouldn't their touch be a welcome thing? Shouldn't our arms be extended fearlessly and unself-consciously?

I wish I could show you the video of that event. The camera captured one moment that repeated itself over and over across the stadium. A boy of about seventeen stood stiffly, arms clamped to his sides, as his father clumsily tried to figure out how to hug his boy.

My heart broke. We crave simple, natural, intimate expressions of love. Why all the awkward hesitation? It was like looking at eighty thousand junior-high boys at their first dance. That's why I tried to help. "Grasp each other by the shoulders," I said. I figured it was a "manlier," easier thing to do. "Tell your son, or tell your father, 'I love you.'"

That's when the dam broke. Words can work miracles. Oh, how I wish you could have heard the sound of eighty thousand people saying those three words. Sons to fathers; fathers to sons: "I love you." The macho pretense of shoulder-grasping was quickly abandoned. The rigid seventeen-year-old and his father stumbled over chairs as they collapsed in each other's arms without shame or embarrassment. Even the day's heat was forgotten; another kind of warmth had blanketed the arena. "Now—pray for each other," I directed.

Prayer one-on-one: This is a moment of intimacy and vulnerability. We take someone's hand and come before the throne of God together. Praying together is a tender expression of trust, forgiveness, and love. Only a misguided sense of pride would hinder us from humbling ourselves before God in each other's presence.

I feel utterly vulnerable when I pray with my wife. She knows my imperfections; she's faced my moments of petty anger and agonizing failure. I can't even remember to lift the toilet lid and put it back down again—how can I join with her to approach a perfect God? I know these men faced the same cautionary considerations, but it didn't matter. The floodgates were open.

They began to pray boldly and with no hesitation. It was one of the most moving and beautiful sounds I'd ever heard—the indescribable music of eighty thousand men praying and expressing love for one another. But as I was taking it all in, a startling sight caught my eye. A middle-aged man sprinted down the center aisle to the ten-foot stage and pulled up just below the platform. He looked up with tears streaming down his face and called up to me, "I lost my father."

I assumed his dad had passed away. I stepped away from the microphone and shouted down my condolences: "I'm so sorry."

"No, no," he responded. "He's not dead—I've lost him!" He gestured wildly in the direction of eighty thousand men. "We've been separated. He's somewhere in the stadium and I want to pray with him."

"You can pray with him later," I shouted reassuringly. When I said those words, the man doubled up and began to weep. Lifting his tearstained face to me, he begged, "Please, I want to say 'I love you' and pray with my dad now! My name is Jeff Williams and my father's name is Henry. Please get him down here!"

How could I ignore such a request? Stepping back to the microphone I said, "Henry Williams, your son Jeff is down here. He loves you and he wants to pray with you right now."

You might suspect this man was some kind of dysfunctional fellow. Think again. When I made the announcement that brought these two together, men and boys who'd been separated from each other came running from all over the stadium. "My name is Bill, my son's name is John—could you please call him?" ... "My name is Richard, please ask my dad ..." And on and on it went.

I couldn't grant all their requests, but I could draw a simple conclusion. Putting a roof over someone's head is a sign of love; staying faithful within a marriage is a sign of love; making a home a comfortable and safe haven is a sign of love. But God's creatures desperately need to be held. They need to feel the reassuring warmth of human touch. They need to hear the words "I love you."

A corny phrase from an old song sums it up: "What the world needs now is love, sweet love." Jesus came to earth and touched us with love. He left a record of his heart that echoes through the ages, saying, "I love you. I love you. I love you." The message never ends. His actions, his words, and his life confirm his love for us. And with the message he left a directive for us to follow:

A new command I give you: Love one another. As I have loved you, so you must love one another. ... And now these three remain: faith, hope and love. But the greatest of these is love.   —*John 13:34 and 1 Corinthians 13:13*

Just a thought:

What the world needs now is still love, sweet love. Say "I love you" to someone today.

What Do You Say to God?

Formal prayer has never come easy for me. As a child I was hesitant to pray aloud, because I didn't know how. I was scolded for praying about "trivial" things, such as a newborn kitten's survival. Prayers were to be properly spoken, and they were reserved for proper things.

I've put aside such childish beliefs, yet I'm still intimidated by those who pray easily in public. I've studied the great lives of prayer. I think about those "sunrise saints" kneeling for long hours, and I'm painfully aware that my own knees are free of bruises.

I've been with people who claim to pray without ceasing, and I've secretly wondered when they prayed and how it affected their lives. I wondered why a few of them weren't pleasant in demeanor at all, but demanding and abrasive. Above all else, I struggled with my own prayer life. I carried with me a sense of guilt that I still didn't know how to pray— that if I enlisted as a prayer warrior, I might not make it through boot camp.

One of my favorite childhood verses always haunted me. It says in 1 Thessalonians 5:17 that we should "pray continually." I liked this verse for the same reason I liked John 11:35: at two words, it's easy to memorize. But it certainly isn't easy to apply. How can I pray all the time? How would I get anything done? Are there really people who pray all the time? These questions took residence in my head when I was a child, and after I grew up they came back for frequent visits.

It took one of our famed family camping trips to open my eyes to what it might mean to pray continually. Diane, the two girls, and I were camping deep in a remote Colorado wilderness when we stumbled upon an outdoor chapel. Long ago someone had discovered a pulpit-shaped rock, arranged a few logs as pews, and fashioned a lovely little setting that inspired spontaneous worship.

We found it entirely by accident. No paths led to it; the nearest road was miles away. It occurred to me that we might be the first folks to come across this work of art, and I felt a sense of awe. I stepped behind the rock pulpit and suggested taking a moment to thank God for the fantastic beauty surrounding us. And I was improvising a little devotional message when Taryn—about four at the time—announced, "I want to preach."

I surrendered the platform and joined Diane and Traci on the log pews. Taryn was wearing a red jacket with a pointed hood. When she stood behind the rock pulpit, all you could see were two eyes and the pointed hood. With a sweeping gesture she began, her squeaky little voice almost lost in the vast forest: "God made all this. He made the trees, he made the rocks, he made the sky." She looked from side to side and gestured toward everything she mentioned.

It seemed the sermon was drawing to a close when a squirrel chirped. Taryn amended, "He made squirrels and stuff." She gazed at the carpet of leaves blanketing the ground and added, "God made the leaves." Again it seemed she had exhausted the inventory of things God made. But the red hood had slipped down over her eyes, and she had to reach up and adjust it. "He made this coat and these hands!" she exclaimed with renewed delight.

From the log pews we could only see chubby little hands gesturing wildly, and two eyes and a hood. I tried to maintain some semblance of reverence, but Traci and Diane lost their composure and began laughing uncontrollably. The stone pulpit suddenly grew silent, and the little preacher stepped out from behind it and impaled her sister with a self-righteous stare.

Pointing her finger at Traci, the tiny pulpiteer spoke: "But there are still sinners in this world. I learned all this from the Bible," she said. "But you don't even read the Bible. You don't even know how God made people!" Taryn was wagging her finger in stern rebuke.

Between gasps for air, Traci asked, "How did God make people, Taryn?"

Taryn homed in on her sinning sister with authority. "First God took some mud," she expounded. "Then he scrunched it up like clay and made the mud into Adam." Taking a deep breath, she continued, "Then he saw that Adam didn't have any friends. So God knocked him out, took out his lungs, and gave them to a woman."

I fell off the log.

Once Taryn recognized we weren't mocking her, she joined in the laughter. Little did she know that she'd taught her father a lesson about praying continually. It wasn't about staying locked in a closet all day. It wasn't even about being on our knees all day. It was about being continually conscious of the Creator's presence—being so intimately in touch with him that we see his hand in everything that happens to us.

We saw a squirrel, but Taryn saw a creation of God. She found joy in it and thanked him for it on the spot. When I reread the verses surrounding the directive to pray continually, what I found was a description of Taryn's actions:

Be joyful always; pray continually; give thanks in all circumstances, for this is God's will for you in Christ Jesus. —1 Thessalonians 5:16–18

Taryn didn't have all the thees and thous of "proper" prayer in order—and it didn't matter in the least. Her heart was in the right place. God doesn't long for us to address him in King James English or, for that matter, proper language of any kind. God longs for us to talk to him— all the time. He doesn't care if we say it incorrectly or if we ask for the wrong things. In a letter to another church, Paul, the one who told us to pray continually, said this about our prayers:

In the same way, the Spirit helps us in our weakness. We do not know what we ought to pray for, but the Spirit himself intercedes for us with groans that words cannot express. And he who searches our hearts knows the mind of the Spirit, because the Spirit intercedes for the saints in accordance with God's will. —Romans 8:26–27

God wants us to ask for what we need. He longs to hear our words of thanks and praise. In a nutshell, God's message to us concerning prayer is simple: "I love you. Please keep in touch."

The Invisible Sweater

Kathy lived in a sad and angry world. Her experience with legalism as a child had left her with painful scars of guilt, self-doubt—and a hatred of pastors.

Kathy knew all about pastors. In her mind they were the self-righteous dispensers of legalism who had left her with jagged scars of guilt and remorse.

In time, her entire demeanor had become a projection of those old wounds. Her life, her words, and her gestures had become one sustained cry for help. Only those of us who loved her could hear her calling out in pain.

I remember the day when Kathy attended the Dynamic Communicators Workshop. Those seminars, of course, are magnets for ministerial types. Kathy knew that. That's why she stood by the door, taking the measure of the auditorium. "I hate pastors," she said, adding a curse for an extra flourish of defiance. She fixed her glare on a tall, distinguished gentleman with snow-white hair and murmured, "Typical preacher! Keep him away from me—I will not be responsible for what I do if he gets too close." She wasn't kidding.

I'd wondered for years how I could break through into Kathy's world. For that matter, I'd wondered if it could even be done. My own universe was brightly illumined by God's healing of broken lives. I lived out the blessing of seeing despair transformed to hope on a regular basis. But for Kathy, real hope seemed unavailable at any price.

Being sensitive to her clerical aversion, I tried to accommodate Kathy by keeping her segregated from the pastors she loathed. But I could never have rearranged enough chairs to block the shrewd, gracious, marvelous maneuvering of God.

Kathy wandered into a room filled nearly to capacity. At that point, two adjoining seats were unfilled. She'd at least have a one-seat Pastor-Free Zone. She made her choice and settled into her place. And as she did so, the distinguished, white-haired pastor she had loathed appeared and claimed the other chair. Her seating assignment was sealed for the duration, yoking her with the living embodiment of ministers everywhere—the

Arch-Pastor himself! The full horror of this dawned on her. I saw the expression that came across her face, but the situation was out of my hands.

I watched curiously as the days and sessions played out. Kathy was a captive audience for dozens of presentations proclaiming the power of God. She heard the stories of lives changed forever by forgiveness. And inevitably, she was called on to interact with those around her. On these occasions she was loved and treated kindly, time after time. The whole experience amounted to a leisurely demolition of her long-held and deeply cherished stereotypes of God and the Christian faith.

None of this is to say that she surrendered without a struggle. On the contrary, she clung tenaciously, willfully, to the fortifications of her biases. But I came to understand the reason God hadn't allowed me to shelter Kathy from the presence of the dreaded white-haired pastor, whose name happened to be Gordon. There she sat—fully disarmed— beside one of the kindest, gentlest spirits I'd ever met. Kathy persisted in treating him coldly; he retaliated just as stubbornly with warmth and kindness. Something had to give.

The x-factor turned out to be Kathy's chain-smoking habit. She was coping with an added layer of tension because the building was "smoke-free." With every break in the sessions, she inevitably bolted for the door in a cold sweat. One day we were finishing a quick stand-and-stretch break when Kathy burst into the building. Short of breath and trailing a cloud of smoke, she ran right into Gordon. "What were you doing?" he asked.

Quite predictably, Kathy fired back a retort fueled by all the criticism and judgment she'd endured over the years. "I was smoking a cigarette," she snapped. "What's it to you?"

Taking her vehemence in stride, the pastor glanced at his watch. "You couldn't have done it justice," he drawled, a huge smile creeping across his face. "You should take a little more time."

Who could have predicted it? This was a nondescript moment; a trivial bit of small talk. Yet some deep, entrenched barrier within Kathy's heart chose that particular moment to begin to give way. In the face of her rude behavior, Gordon's simple goodness prevailed. Without even trying, he broke through to her world by accepting her just the way she was—by loving her despite her inability to love back.

Gordon's goodwill punched a small hole in the great dam she'd been constructing, at tremendous emotional expense, for decades. The dam had held back the rivers of God's care for her. It had pushed back the currents of concern that flowed from those who loved her. Most of all,

Kathy's dam had stifled her magnificent potential to love others. And now the dam was breached, once and for all.

The hole in the dam only grew in the aftermath. When her turn came to give a speech on a topic of her choice, Kathy offered up a heartrending exercise in vulnerability titled "Snake or Savior?" She laid bare her terror of reaching out to God for fear of being bitten one more time. Her soul, she explained, could bear no further scar.

The floodgates fully opened. Kathy finally did what had seemed unthinkable just a day or two earlier; she placed her trust in the only One who could heal her bruised heart. She faced her Maker honestly, willingly, and without reservation.

The transformation was instantaneous and dramatic. When she returned to her job, her coworkers didn't recognize her. She looked younger and carried herself more lightly. Anger and bitterness had been erased from her face. Kathy was at peace, but that was only the beginning. Her marriage flourished and grew.

Today Kathy has become what she once dreaded. She is the pastor of a small church on the East Coast. She teaches at the same workshop where God's love finally and tumultuously broke through in her life. Among those fortunate enough to enter the realm of her ministry, she demonstrates an uncanny gift of reaching beyond the aching defenses of life's walking wounded. The embittered Kathy who hurled stones at every Christian in sight is gone forever. The Kathy of today is a joyful spirit who lavishes time and love on the elderly and dying. And she speaks passionately to audiences about the power of reaching people by loving them where they are; the adventure of entering the worlds of people like Helen—a story that always captivates our seminar audience. Listen to her for a moment:

"I met Helen," Kathy begins, "when she was 101 years old. She was my hospice patient for months. They finally kicked her out of the program when she turned 102 because she was doing too well to qualify. That's Helen all over. The last I heard, she was celebrating her 103d birthday.

"Helen was one of the most joyful people I've ever known. This elderly saint had a gentle, laughing spirit. She was alert and conversant, delighting in our visits.

"But Helen's reality was not our reality; she lived in a world of her own. The people who populated her days were people I couldn't see or hear. They were ghosts from her past—old memories who'd come to life again for Helen.

"I knew I had both feet in the real world. I asked myself how I could somehow meet Helen in that special place in which she lived. I had to learn how to step through the portal into her world.

"One day, as my son and I were visiting with Helen, she picked up some cloth that was invisible to us. She straightened her needle and thread, neither of which we could see—and she began to sew a phantom sweater in meticulously perfect stitches.

"She smiled brightly as we discussed the delicacy of the fabric and the neat rows of thread. But her hands apparently became clumsy. She dropped the sewing needle. Then my son and I were down on the floor on our hands and knees, peering under tables and chairs. We found ourselves joining in the search for a needle that existed only in Helen's mind.

"Helen's world had indeed become ours. That's why I'm wearing tonight, in Helen's honor, the sweater she made me . . ."

At this point, Kathy turns slowly, 360 degrees, to show us a sweater that doesn't exist. Or does it? There's no thread or cloth; no buttons or collar. It's a mantle of grace and love that enfolds Kathy. It's sewn of a supernatural fiber rugged enough to change a hateful heart to one willing to crawl on the floor in search of an invisible needle, for no other purpose than to enter the world of an elderly woman with a small portion of God's love.

As Kathy turns round and round on the stage, we see no sweater at all. But those of us who know her can plainly make out the mantle. It floods the room with dazzling light as she smiles; it captures our hearts with every shining tear that drips down her cheek. As she continues to turn, we recognize the mantle; our clothing is knitted of the same fabric. Someone has reached into our private worlds to touch us with Jesus' love, and to drape that warm mantle across our shoulders.

Just a thought:

It was Gordon who finally got through to Kathy. It was Kathy who reached into Helen's world. Whom will you touch today?

I See a Ducky and a Horsey

The movie is *Good Will Hunting,* an Academy Award-winner. The scene plays out between an MIT professor and a young student. The boy doesn't have any formal training, but he's a bona fide genius—so much so that it provokes an identity crisis for the professor. In one powerful scene, the instructor stumbles to his knees, clutching a math problem he's incapable of solving. This kid has handled with ease what the older man, with his consummate training, could not. The professor's entire self-concept is called into question; he feels diminished and devastated.

I see myself in that character. Feelings of inadequacy often overwhelm and paralyze me. Such moments come without warning and affect the very core of my being. I realize I'd be considered successful by the world's standards—after all, I've written seven books; I've traveled the world and appeared on stage and television. I've attained a measure of notoriety in some circles. I have more requests for personal appearances than I can possibly accommodate. I live in a comfortable home where my basic needs are met. You might suspect these things would mean an inflated ego and an expanded hat size.

Nothing could be further from the truth. Throughout this book I've shared my weaknesses with you—but I wouldn't list an inflated ego among those flaws. Public visibility doesn't always imply conceit. If our accomplishments are the measure of our worth, then we're all with that MIT math professor, stumbling to our knees on shifting sands. There will always be someone who's gone farther and accomplished more.

Several years ago I was invited to join a small group comprised of men and women in visible public ministry. The group was created to establish a safe community for mutual accountability. We met monthly and sought to challenge each other to a closer walk with God.

From the moment I received the invitation, I felt like the odd man out. Members of the group included best-selling authors, Ph.D. degree holders, a nationally renowned psychologist, and the executive producer of one of the nation's most powerful radio ministries. The president of a large national ministry to women, the founder of a high-tech Internet educational program, and the manager of a hospice-care center were also included.

Oh, and me—a guy without a formal education who makes people laugh while communicating truth. During some of our discussions, I felt like Charlie Brown in that "Peanuts" cartoon in which the characters are lying on the ground watching clouds. "That cloud looks like a reproduction of Rembrandt's 'The Night Watch,'" observes Lucy.

"I see Michelangelo's 'David,'" says Linus. "What do you see, Charlie Brown?"

Charlie Brown hesitates. "I was going to say I saw a ducky and a horsey, but never mind."

Our group is filled with brilliant people with spectacular gifts. Each has been extremely successful in his or her career. Over and over, these kindred spirits have affirmed me and honored the value of my unique gifts. Yet each time a discussion takes them to the edge of some deep philosophical chasm; each time they discuss the marketing strategy for their sophisticated products; each time they display their knowledge of the Bible or their rigorous thought processes—I cringe with a deep sense of inferiority.

After one group discussion, a brilliant author and academician acknowledged and encouraged my thinking process. He went out of his way to thank me for my discernment. His comments gave me hope that I might indeed have a functioning brain. Yet as I sat through *Good Will Hunting* and watched that mathematician kneeling in despair, my own feelings of inadequacy came flooding back.

I watch John Elway win two Super Bowls, then score in the top ten of a celebrity golf tournament. Why couldn't God have given him his football skills and automobile dealerships—and given me the golf ability? (Okay, I'd settle for the automobile dealerships.) Yet I forget—there are things I can do that John Elway will never accomplish.

I'm amazed I'm not the only person to suffer from this malady. It turns out that everyone in our group struggles with inadequacy pangs. Some even covet my gift of humor. Some feel their abilities are too meager for the scope of their ministries. With great accomplishments, it would seem, comes great insecurity.

Why can't I just rejoice in the success of others? Instead I stand their achievements on end, make a pencil mark, then measure mine against theirs—and I come up short every time. When God asked us not to covet, I think he meant not just our neighbors' wives and donkeys, but their gifts as well.

There's only one yardstick by which to measure our worth. You and I were made in the image of God. Whatever attributes and giftedness he's given us is a reflection of God himself. Your combination of giftedness is absolutely unique. Mine is exceptionally weird. There's none other like either of us in the universe.

Here's a list of personal reminders I use:

I will never play golf like Tiger Woods.
I will never play football and live to tell about it.
I will never be the wordsmith my friend and best-selling author is.
I will never change the world with my deep philosophical contributions.
I will never get the lead role in *Titanic*.
I will never beat my mother in a game of cards.

Here is the most important fact concerning the above:

IT DOESN'T MATTER.

Then why, I ask, does my mind herd all those negative thoughts together and nurture them? Here is all that matters:

God made me in his image.
God made me unique.
God loves me.

We are significant because our Creator is significant, and he has perfectly equipped us to make a dent in this world. You are the only one who can make the unique contribution he put you on earth to make.

It doesn't matter how much we get paid for doing it. It doesn't matter whether the world recognizes what we've done. How much you contribute in comparison to me doesn't matter. All that matters is that we be everything God created us to be. He never intended us to be like someone else.

If he's pleased with what he created, then why should we compare ourselves to other persons? Why should we feel inadequate to serve him? I'm still learning that God doesn't make junk. Now he wants us to trust him enough to believe it. It's really all God asks.

I praise you because I am fearfully and wonderfully made; your works are wonderful, I know that full well. My frame was not hidden from you when I was made in the secret place. When I was woven together in the depths of the earth, your eyes saw my unformed body. All the days ordained for me were written in your book before one of them came to be. How precious to me are your thoughts, O God! How vast is the sum of them! Were I to count them, they would outnumber the grains of sand. When I awake, I am still with you. —Psalm 139:14–18

Falling in Love Again

When I first realized there was a problem, Diane and I were sitting at the dinner table. It was only two weeks since our youngest daughter had left home, and an uncomfortable silence had fallen across our empty nest.

Our home had never been a silent one. With two daughters there were always the sounds of quarreling or excited boyfriend-chatter. There'd always been whining or laughter or the muffled rhythm of private phone conversations. And where the talking ended, the music began—head-splitting, mind-numbing, window-rattling music.

But now it was quiet. Now it was only Diane and me, and the only sound was the scraping of my fork pushing peas around the plate. Something was wrong. We'd worked together all our lives. Now that the kids were gone, work-related dialogue had expanded to fill the void of silence.

But the silence of this evening signaled an uncomfortable truth: Diane and I had managed to grow out of touch with each other. We had allowed intimacy to be pushed aside by business and the busyness of raising children. Without knowing it, somewhere along the line we'd stopped growing deep together. The evening silence didn't seem sinister—it just felt uneasy and empty.

I met Diane at Bible college. I'd always thought of her as a nice girl, but I wasn't attracted to her until one day in December of 1966. We worked together peeling potatoes to help pay for our education. On that fateful day, as Diane reached into the huge vat of potatoes, her glasses fell off. She wore the ugliest pair of glasses on the face of the earth. The frames of the glasses had that bird-wing shape—very stylish in the early sixties. Why they were designed that way I'll never know. They made the wearer look as if her face might fly away at any moment.

Up to this moment I hadn't paid any attention to Diane's glasses other than to wonder what would happen to her face in a strong wind. Without her glasses, Diane couldn't see into the murky potato-water. "Would you get them for me?" she asked.

I could see them lying at the bottom of the vat like some transparent prehistoric raptor. I handed them to her, my arm dripping with potato-water. Then I saw her eyes. I yanked my hand back and said, "Look at me."

"I can't even see you until I have my glasses on," she pleaded.

"Then just let me look at you," I crooned. (How suave it sounds as I write it now. Why is it that romantic lines come so easily in early courtship—and so slowly when you're eating peas in an empty house thirty years later?)

I'd never seen such beautiful eyes. Diane had to earn her wings that day: I wouldn't give them back until she promised to go out with me. She got her glasses, and I got a date. Blindness is a powerful motivator.

The year ahead was filled with the wonderful rituals of courtship: long walks, soul-baring conversations, creative gifts that said, "I love you." We discussed our future and shared our dreams. We exchanged passionate kisses and passionate prayer. I fell in love with this gentle, beautiful creature, and on May 4, 1968, we were married.

My love for Diane is greater today than the day I said "I do." What had happened? Why was our table so silent? I'm not suggesting that the passion of thirty years ago should have continued with the same intensity as when I was twenty. If it had, with my cholesterol level, I would have died of heart failure years ago. But something was missing on that night of the silent table. A vital link. And so we talked late into the night. We committed ourselves to spending intimate time together away from the office. We needed to play together, pray together, and reconnect our souls.

Shortly after that pea-shuffling evening when the silence had brought us to our senses, Diane said, "Date me."

Being a man, my first thought was, "Why? We're already married."

Before we were married, I dated Diane to get to know her better and to convince her to marry me. Now she wanted me to date her so I could know her more fully, love her more deeply, and show her more convincingly that my love was a living thing.

Our love, we learned, is alive and well. I agreed to date her—but only if she promised to leave her wings at home.

In churches, marriages, and parenting, it's too easy to speed up living and slow down loving. We go to church where we sing the hymns and listen to the message and give the money. In all the commotion we miss the voice of Jesus, who says, "Remember me? I love you. I miss you. Church is about you and me getting to know each other better." Jesus isn't listed anywhere in the bulletin. But he's what church is all about.

We talk constantly to our children. "Have you put out the garbage? Is your homework done? What's that growing on your teeth?" In the process we often miss their unspoken cry: "Do you love me? Are you proud of me? Do you care about my hurts, my fears, and my dreams?" Their names probably don't appear in your daily planner, but loving them is what you're all about.

Lighten up your relationship with your spouse, and deepen it at the same time. Don't let the passion slip from your life; fan the flames of love for your family and for the God who loves you. Do more than conduct family business. Break the silence; say "I love you."

Ralph and the Nine Nasties

When I was a child, true religion was a list of Nine Nasties every good boy avoided. Playing cards was among the Arch-Nasties. Each card was supposedly a demonic symbol with the power to condemn the soul to eternal torment. Even today I can hear the gates of Hades begin to creak open at the sound of a shuffling deck.

I was told that card playing meant irrevocable damage to my testimony. Even such innocent diversions as Old Maid were taboo. The reasoning went like this: Someone might peek in the window, see the backs of the cards, and assume you were using the regular demonic deck. And Old Maid fell under the category of "avoiding the appearance of evil."

Cards were only the beginning of the slippery slope to purgatory. One dance step and you'd be dancing your way to the fiery pit. You did not pass go. You did not collect two hundred dollars. It was ballroom to brimstone, plain and simple. Didn't it say somewhere in the holy Scriptures that praying knees were never connected to dancing feet?

We used to whisper about the impropriety of making love standing up—God might think you were dancing. Even when singing hymns, you avoided rhythmic movement. Turning bodies became burning bodies.

I hope you're not about to throw the book across the room. I'm neither condemning nor endorsing any of the above; I'm trying to make a broader point. Christianity isn't defined by a list of taboos. Yet some Christians place all their emphasis on a short, convenient set of perceived sins to avoid, rather than on a vibrant relationship with a living Savior.

The rule of thumb in my community went like this: If you don't drink, if you don't smoke, if you don't chew, if you don't go to the theater, if you don't play cards, and if you don't dance, then you're a good Christian.

Each denomination and subdenomination had its own variation of the Nine Nasties. Some took it to extremes that challenged the rational mind. When she was a little girl, Diane was told that lipstick was made of snakes' blood. Nylon stockings were the shed skins of the Serpent—not just any serpent, but The Serpent with a capital T and a capital S.

Speaking of snakes, playing any game that required the use of dice was strictly *verboten*. Didn't you know why the single dots on the dice were called "snake eyes"? Nylons, lipstick, and dice came from a common source with a strong smell of sulfur.

At about the age of eleven, I had a unique experience. I was sitting on the porch frying ants with a magnifying glass and contemplating the deeper aspects of snake theology. Ralph, my collie dog, walked by. Suddenly I had a revelation: Ralph didn't smoke, drink, or play cards; nor did he wear nylons or lipstick. If avoiding those activities defined a Christian, then Ralph was a better Christian than I was. I'd never succumbed to the temptation to wear lipstick or nylons, but Lord knows I'd experimented with gin rummy behind closed doors.

If Christianity is defined by what we don't do, then the best Christians on the planet are mannequins. They don't do anything—including touch anyone's life. You'll never see a TV documentary about a mannequin's profound influence on society.

I've visited countries in the Middle East where the taboo list includes all the snaky trespasses listed above, plus a whole extra list. Breaking the rules in some of these countries can literally cost you an arm and a leg. These people don't even profess to be Christians, but they can out-forbid us any day.

There's a great temptation to point to an empty dance card as evidence of devotion and faith. And some of us "sophisticated" souls have our own, more modern, lists. I know a few mean-spirited, even hateful people whose entire faith is limited to avoiding the Nine Nasties or some other scrupulous code of behavior. Because their focus is so narrow, they're blinded to their own un-Christlike attitudes. They're about as effective as the mannequin in touching a love-starved world.

It's living, breathing, occasionally stumbling lovers of Jesus Christ who make a difference in this world. Yes, most assuredly strong faith does lead to good conduct—and there are many things that are prudent to avoid. But God's list of behavioral commandments is relatively short, and it's written in stone. His Word makes one thing clear: Obedience to those commandments isn't the mark of a Christian; it's simply a by-product of the new life we have in Jesus Christ, as we show by our deeds that we are thankful to God for all he has done for us.

Just a thought:

The genuine mark of a believer is love—love for each other and for the Father. All other Christian behavior flows naturally from the love we receive from God and the gratitude we express as a result of what God has done for us.

Ralph hasn't even got a clue about that.

Jesus replied: "Love the Lord your God with all your heart and with all your soul and with all your mind." This is the first and greatest commandment. And the second is like it: "Love your neighbor as yourself." All the Law and the Prophets hang on these two commandments.
—Matthew 22:37

The Right Place at the Right Time

Do you ever wonder if God is really involved in your everyday life? Does it seem like miracles and direct answers to prayer only happen in other people's lives?

God is always working in your life and mine; we're simply not aware of it most of the time. His angels remain invisible. But once in a great while, he shows his hand for one brief, shining moment. He gives us a glimpse behind the scenes—a burning bush to reassure us of his grace-filled presence.

I awoke on October 19 with a full day ahead of me. I was scheduled to speak at 1:30 in the ballroom of the Indianapolis Convention Center. The title of my talk was "A Wimpy Prophet, a Butane Bush, and No Excuses." It was a simple message about God's call to Moses and the lame excuses he put forth to try to get off the hook. Most of us think of Moses as the Charlton Heston-type—handsome, courageous, and eager for the challenge. The Bible paints another picture entirely.

When God appeared to Moses in a bush and told him to lead the Israelites out of slavery, Moses tried every excuse in the book to avoid being used: He didn't feel qualified; he wanted God to directly intervene. "Who am I for such a task?" he groaned.

Most of us try that one when God calls us. "Who, me? I'm just a nobody," we moan.

Moses figured God should come up with a better-qualified candidate—someone extraordinary. But God isn't looking for extraordinary people. He's looking for ordinary people who trust an extraordinary God. When Moses complained that he wasn't capable, God's response was, "I'll go with you."

The man wasn't convinced. "I don't know what to say," Moses whined.

Things are no different today. I've heard that excuse countless times. I've even used it myself. But God doesn't expect us to have all the right words memorized. Surely we should be prepared. But when the chips are down, God will use our weaknesses to accomplish his will. God told Moses exactly what to say. He has the right words for you and me too.

Despite God's amazing promises, Moses continued his relentless efforts to evade responsibility. "What if they don't believe me?" he moaned. Charlton Heston was the wrong person to play Moses in *The Ten Commandments*. Martin Short should have had that role. He'd have been perfect.

God answered the question with a demonstration. Wouldn't you love to have seen Moses' face when he threw down his shepherd's staff and it turned into a snake? Can you imagine his expression when he picked it up and it turned back into a stick?

Memo to Moses: It's not your job to make people believe—that's God's department.

So what's our job? Simply to be faithful in proclaiming the truth. God promised to go with Moses. God gave him the exact words; God even displayed miraculous signs for making the Egyptians believe—and still Moses dug in his heels: "I don't speak very well," he stammered.

God's response: "Who made your lips?" The lesson is clear. God had equipped Moses perfectly for the job ahead. In his hands, our disabilities become possibilities.

Finally, in desperation, Moses cried out, "Send someone else." According to the Bible, God's face now burned with anger. He didn't want someone else; he wanted Moses.

"And he wants you." That's the challenge I threw out to my audience. "Has God made you aware of a call or a task that you've been avoiding?" I asked. "Which of Moses' excuses are you using? Is it, 'I'm a nobody'? God will go with you. You and God together are a team that can't be beaten.

"Are you complaining that you don't know what to say? God had the words for Moses, and he has the words for you.

"Are you worried they won't believe you? That's not your job.

"Are you convinced you aren't physically or mentally equipped? God has perfectly equipped you for whatever he calls you to do.

"God wants you," I concluded. "What's your response?"

Gary Ballard awoke early that same morning. The successful businessman hadn't slept well at all. He'd been receiving a call from God—one just as clear as a burning bush. Gary was being called to become a pastor. Like Moses before him, Gary had tried every excuse in the book. But he couldn't sleep the previous night, nor could he get the voice of God out of his head.

Gary rose, put on his clothes, and drove into Indianapolis to get some coffee. He parked his car several blocks from the downtown area and began to walk. He had no specific destination in mind; he just wanted to clear his head of the persistent prodding of God's Spirit. Gary walked through the revolving door of the Weston Hotel, knowing there'd be a coffee shop somewhere inside. He walked past the registration desk, missed the coffee shop, and found himself in a covered walkway that connects the Weston to the Indianapolis Convention Center.

Gary kept walking. Perhaps he could get some coffee in the convention center. As he approached the end of the walkway, he heard the laughter of four thousand people radiating from one of the auditoriums. Gary Ballard stepped into the room the very instant I began my talk about Moses.

At the conclusion of my presentation, I stepped just offstage to greet those waiting to talk with me. But I caught a glimpse of a lone figure on the periphery. He was waiting until the others had left, and he caught my eye because he was weeping.

At 1:35 in the afternoon on October 19, God had caused the paths of two people to intersect—two people from different walks of life. He'd led Gary to this spot to hear a message that would change his life. He'd led me there not only to deliver the message, but also to catch a glimpse of a burning bush.

It was approximately 3:30 when the last person left and Gary stepped up with tears streaming from his face. His words were right to the point: "Several months ago, God made it clear to me that he wanted me in the ministry," he confessed. "I didn't want to give up my business; I didn't feel qualified for the job. I've been using exactly the same excuses Moses used."

Gary continued. "Today God led me clear across town, through a hotel and a convention complex. I was drawn by the laughter. Then I stood in the back of the room, unable to move as I listened to your message. I've been making excuses and running from God," he said through his tears. "But I'm not going to run anymore."

Now we were both weeping and laughing. We'd seen the burning bush. God had made his presence known to both of us. He'd gotten our attention.

God's hand is constantly working in our lives. Every day he guides us to safety, brings people we need into our lives, and orchestrates events that demonstrate his love. It was God's hand that led Gary on a wandering quest for coffee. We were both privileged to see visible evidence of the hand of God in our lives.

You may not always be aware of his influence, but never doubt his activity.

Just a thought:

When God gets your attention—pay attention. There are no excuses that can stand up in the presence of our all-powerful, infinitely capable God.

How to Kill a Grizzly Bear

I was more than exhausted.

In the last twenty-four hours I'd flown two thousand miles, driven two hundred miles, spent three hours in airports, and delivered two speeches. I was functioning on less than two hours of sleep, and there was no rest in sight.

I'd just had one of those endless nights dueling with the hotel room air conditioner. The air conditioner won. Apparently the blades in the unit's fan were bent; either that or a tiny version of the Indianapolis 500 was being run within my room's cooling unit. With each start-up, I heard the distinct sounds of a multicar collision followed by spinning hubcaps and twisting metal.

I knew the routine by heart, from too many nights in too many hotels. First came the grinds and grunts of the ancient unit straining to kick into gear. Then the blades would slam and scrape against the metal walls until the centrifugal force lifted them sufficiently to clear the runway—I had plenty of time to figure out all the high-school physics of that while the shrieking metal was relieving me of various stages of slumber.

About that time the thermostat would drop sufficiently to shut off the air. The blades would clank and crank their way to an exhausted halt. I'd achieve a moment or two of blessed silence before the grinds and grunts would return to proclaim a whole new cycle. Under such circumstances my reactions are predictable, just as the reactions of a grizzly bear are predictable when his hibernation is disrupted.

I spoke twice the next morning, then raced to the airport. Because of a last-minute flight change by the airline, we'd touch down just about the starting time of my next engagement—and the airport was an hour away. Needless to say, my host was less than pleased with the tight scheduling.

I wasn't too delighted myself. Stumbling through the airport, I was more interested in blissful hibernation than in hitting the stage with a high-energy, humorous, and inspiring talk. I was growling to myself, grizzly-style, about lack of sleep and food. I was smelling grizzly-style, too, in the same clothes I'd thrown on early that morning. I was not a happy bear.

I was speaking to KCARC, a group dedicated to serving individuals with disabilities. About one hundred of the four hundred attendees had some form of disability, whether mental or physical. A short awards ceremony was just beginning as I arrived. While the awards were being handed out, I noticed constant movement among those in the audience; many of them needed assistance to get to the rest room. And as the presenters offered their comments, I heard the involuntary moans and vocal sounds echoing throughout the audience.

Everyone else in the room seemed to handle all this casually and politely—a simple matter of routine. But not the veteran grizzly. He found himself criticizing the lighting. He grumbled about the quality of the sound system. He growled quietly about the noise and movement and how they might disrupt his talk. Above all, he longed for a comfy, hibernation-friendly cave somewhere—with a well-mannered air conditioner.

As I was grimly ruminating on these things, the presenters called Andrew Roach to come to the platform. I watched a beautiful seven-year-old boy make his way forward to accept his award. And what was Andrew's achievement? Over the past year, we were told, he'd learned to sit in his seat long enough to complete a task. He'd learned to count to fifty without help. His smile was several miles wide as he clutched his award and returned to his seat. The pride in his parents' eyes was plain to see. And all this for counting to fifty and staying in a seat—I wasn't thinking so much about the lighting now.

The next award was for Resident of the Year. Terry Moreland was sitting only a few feet from the platform, yet it took him almost a full minute to get there. His body is bent from cerebral palsy with spastic dystonic quadriplegia. He can only make halting progress with the use of a walking stick. Each step requires an excruciating effort. I know his one-minute journey seemed like an eternity to me.

Yet the people in the room were not concerned about the delay. Nor did I observe any impatience or tension during the moments when a photographer fumbled with his camera to take a picture. All I saw was a beaming smile that lit up the entire room as Terry stood with his award, waiting for his picture to be taken. I'd been worrying about the lighting for my presentation. Now I realized I didn't need it; at least I didn't need any state-of-the-art, computer-driven spotlight. Only the light of a smile like Andrew's or Terry's was bright enough to break through and illuminate the darkness I was cultivating in my soul that morning.

After the flash, those in charge huddled and conferred. Terry had asked to say a few words. It took another twenty seconds for him to cover the fifteen feet to the podium. But why was I counting? Nobody cared. Terry's fine, strong voice contradicted the bent and crippled condition of the body from which it came. I might have closed my eyes and pictured a graceful, handsome athlete speaking into the microphone. He smiled and offered a few simple words that slew a grizzly that day—right through the heart.

"I want to thank you for this award," he said. "And I want to thank God for another day."

The audience rose in a thunderous ovation as Terry laboriously made his way back to his seat. I wasn't counting the seconds it took this time. I was standing, applauding wildly as I considered deeper things.

Mr. Rosenberg received the next award. He'd run a clothing store in the town of Vincennes for forty-six years. He and his wife were receiving a plaque of recognition for donating his store's old building to KCARC. Marshall, his disabled adult son, accompanied him to the front. What had inspired the generous gift? His voice breaking with emotion, Mr. Rosenberg told us Marshall had recently given him one of the most precious gifts a father could receive. Shortly after becoming a resident of KCARC's residential program, Marshall had blessed his father with two simple but profound words: "I'm happy!" The grizzly bear was dead—and a teddy bear was born.

I began to wonder who it was that was disabled. I'm healthy. I have a wonderful job that I love. I make a good living and lack no material thing. My family is healthy and whole. And on that day my spirit had groaned from nothing more than a hectic and tiring schedule. I had preoccupied myself with the trivial concerns of lighting and acoustics—while somewhere, in this same world, there was Terry, a person who possessed the simple grace to thank God for another day.

I was capable of waking to the sound of rain, pouting because I couldn't play golf—while a retired shopkeeper named Mr. Rosenberg could find deep joy and gratitude simply in hearing his son say, "I'm happy."

Just before it was my turn to speak, I leaned over to my host and whispered, "No message I could deliver would be more inspirational than what I've just heard."

Just a thought:

The next morning, as I awoke, I acted on the lesson I'd learned the night before. The first words from my mouth were these: "Thank you, God, for another day. I am happy."

Show Me the Miracle!

When I was a child, I prayed for God to reveal himself to me through a miracle. Once I even asked him to move our house—four feet to my left. Since then I've often wondered if I would have been satisfied if God had moved it four feet to his own left. I told my mother and she scolded me: "You could have caused an earthquake."

Another time I asked him to change the moon into the sun just long enough for me to see it happen. Given what I know now, it's frightening to consider that I could have been responsible for frying the earth.

Have you ever wished you could see a real, knock-the-wind-out-of-your-sails miracle? I don't mean the kind that can be explained by other means. For example, was the life saved by medicine or by divine intervention? Was the city saved from conflagration by a random shift of the wind, or by God's hand? I'm talking about miracles that can only be explained by divine intervention.

People speak of miracles that sound more like parlor tricks. A woman claims God healed her windshield after it was cracked by a rock. I guess I'm a bit suspicious of claims like that. I notice there's never a second witness, and I find myself wondering if it's just the windshield that's cracked. I'm troubled by the triviality of God healing a broken windshield while millions of humans face gut-wrenching problems.

Some people say my lack of faith keeps me from witnessing a miracle. But I had plenty of faith when I asked God for a four-foot house shift.

Perhaps we're looking in the wrong place. Even as I watch for God to move the floor or fix my flat tire, miracles are actually taking place all around me. They may not be as instantaneous or dramatic as I might ask for, but they're much more spectacular.

I remember receiving a phone call from a young man who'd made a public profession of faith in Jesus Christ. He was struggling with a specific problem in his life and was not, as he put it, "getting the victory." One year after his profession of faith, he was discouraged. He was asking whether God even existed. Where were the signs of God's work in his life anyway?

I tried to point out to him what he couldn't see. He'd been staring at the floor of his life, waiting for the foundation to move four feet to the left. He wanted to feel the earth move under his feet, or the sky to come a-tumblin' down. All the while he was missing the miracle God was accomplishing all around him.

"Why did you call me?" I asked.

"Because I'm dissatisfied with my progress as a believer," he responded. A year ago he didn't even know how to spell "believer." A year ago he didn't care about progress in his life. A year ago he wouldn't have given the problem he was facing a second thought; he wouldn't have considered it a problem. His phone call was a miracle in itself. It was convincing evidence that God had brought him a long way—and surely wasn't done with him yet.

One dark day, at the end of a long struggle with depression, I doubted my own life was worth living. I was disgusted with my failures. What was there about me that God could possibly love? That day I closed the door to a small room with no intention of ever coming out. God flooded my darkness with light, and he pulled off the miracle using only a simple verse written on a piece of construction paper: "We love because he first loved us" (1 John 4:19).

Suddenly I understood. I was loved, I was forgiven, and life was definitely worth living.

The greatest miracle on earth is a changed life. And that truth isn't limited to those radical, high-drama testimonies we hear. It also applies to lives moved a few feet off their foundation.

I know myself well enough to comprehend the power required to make even a small change in my life. Through the years God has brought me through times of failure, a life-threatening bout with depression, and far enough to offer encouragement to you today—and that's a more significant miracle than a whole row of houses moved an entire block.

Just a thought:

You're welcome to the healed windshields and the mysteriously filled teeth. But the greatest miracle on earth is a changed life. Let God do the greatest miracle in your life today.

Leave It There

Kathy Colebank is the dedicated pastor of a wonderful Presbyterian congregation. This church is her first calling. She serves alone, and there have been times she has felt overwhelmed by the responsibility.

Kathy also happens to be my sister. Not too long ago we talked on the phone, and I poured out my soul to her. I told of how I lay awake at night agonizing over my responsibilities. Never mind the heavy burdens my dear sister was facing—I needed encouragement, and I needed it now.

Want to know what kind of heart she has? After I finished moaning and groaning about the unfair burdens it was my lot to carry, the first words out of her mouth weren't words of advice, rebuke, or sympathy. "I love you," she said. "We're so much alike. Can I read something to you?"

She'd written the following piece as she struggled to find a refuge from the unrelenting demands she faced. On the day she penned this, she was fretting over a place to study; a place to prepare for what God had called her to do. See if this touches a chord in your life:

I have a wonderful place in town. It's a place I turn to for intense study, planning, and prayer.

There was a day when I arrived at that destination feeling like a pack mule. I had bags hanging from every bone in my upper body. There was a bag of books and a bag for my laptop computer. There were my purse, a bag lunch, and a cup of coffee. I struggled up the stairs to my favorite workroom, banging into walls and tables with my burdens.

The door was closed. That meant it was already in use. I stood there, draped with the many vestments of professional productivity, my mouth gaping in amazement. How could my dearest work refuge be closed to me? I gently pushed the door open. The table where I loved to work was buried by someone's papers, deep and disheveled. I stood for several seconds, my bones creaking, and turned toward the building's chapel.

I contemplated bringing my professional productivity into the chapel. I thought to myself, "I'll just take it in and bless it. I'll ask God to make it work for me." After considering this for a moment, I thought it best to leave my things right outside the door—in, but not in. I couldn't let myself get too far away from them, you know. One by one I peeled them off: books, computer, purse, lunch, and coffee.

Then I walked into the chapel. I sat down to pray, painfully aware of the throbbing in my shoulders and back—those things are really heavy. I bowed my head in prayer. But the pain in my shoulders wouldn't diminish, and my thoughts kept returning to my aching muscles. As I began to lay before the Lord the burdens on my heart, the big picture began to drift into focus.

I was carrying the accoutrements of my ministry by my neck and shoulders as a yoke. And the shoulders of my ministry were aching as much as those of flesh and bone. I carried the weight of the world on my shoulders, searching for that favorite room where I could lay them all down and set to work fixing them. I came to a new realization: I'd come to believe that somewhere, deep within me, it was *my* job to carry those heavy weights around, that it was *my* responsibility to fix them all.

I bowed and brought myself to hand over each of those things to their rightful owner: God.

"Here's the sermon, Lord. What are we going to do with it?"

"Here's the pain of that person you sent to me yesterday. What are we going to do with it?

"Here's . . ." The list went on and on.

Afterward, I stood and walked to the door of the chapel. I gazed for a moment at the great pile of stuff waiting to be loaded onto my shoulders. "Oh well," I thought. "Here goes." I picked them up one by one, and I slogged off to find a new room in which to work. It was still hard to believe that someone had taken my favorite place. I'd love to tell you I walked out of that chapel free as a bird. I didn't. I don't give things up easily.

But I felt lighter knowing I wasn't walking alone. I believe it will take a long time of giving back—of asking God to teach me to give things back—before I really let them go.

I find myself returning to Kathy's words, "I don't give things up easily." How perfectly she has described her brother; maybe she has described you as well. The things I don't give up easily are the very same things I'm so tired of carrying. They're the chattering monkeys of worry and fear that cling tenaciously to my back, draining my energy and dragging me down. Why would I ever continue to carry them? My anxiety does nothing to alleviate my problems; it only serves to make me less effective in facing them. It is, indeed, a lack of trust. *I trust you, Lord. I really believe you're in control. But I'm going to worry anyway.* Translation: *I don't trust you, Lord.*

At camp we used to sing a song that had this chorus:

> Leave it there. Leave it there.
> Take your burden to the Lord
> and leave it there.
> If you trust and never doubt,
> He will surely bring you out,
> Take your burden to the Lord
> and leave it there.

If it sounds repetitive, that's because it needs to be. My tendency is to:

> Bring 'em back. Bring 'em back.
> Take my burdens to the Lord
> And bring 'em back.

My singular desire in writing these stories was to bring you hope that might lighten the burdens you face. The smiles and tears you've experienced will help only momentarily. It's the truth behind the stories that brought the emotions to the surface. That same truth is the source of hope for both of us. That truth is the light at the end of the tunnel.

Here's the truth:

Therefore I tell you, do not worry about your life, what you will eat or drink; or about your body, what you will wear. Is not life more important than food, and the body more important than clothes? Look at the birds of the air; they do not sow or reap or store away in barns, and yet your heavenly Father feeds them. Are you not much more valuable than they? Who of you by worrying can add a single hour to his life?

And why do you worry about clothes? See how the lilies of the field grow. They do not labor or spin. Yet I tell you that not even Solomon in all his splendor was dressed like one of these. If that is how God clothes the grass of the field, which is here today and tomorrow is thrown into the fire, will he not much more clothe you, O you of little faith? So do not worry, saying, "What shall we eat?" or "What shall we drink?" or "What shall we wear?" For the pagans run after all these things, and your heavenly Father knows that you need them. But seek first his kingdom and his righteousness, and all these things will be given to you as well. Therefore do not worry about tomorrow, for tomorrow will worry about itself. Each day has enough trouble of its own. —Matthew 6:25–34

Why not today? Take your burden to the Lord and *leave it there*. Okay, leave *most* of it there. Okay, leave *something* there.

At least be like Kathy: Ask God to begin teaching you how to lighten up. He's up to the task.

Just a thought:

God is up to the task.

Now to him who is able to do immeasurably more than all we ask or imagine, according to his power that is at work within us, to him be glory in the church and in Christ Jesus throughout all generations, for ever and ever! Amen. —Ephesians 3:20–21

Ken Davis is one of the most sought-after speakers in North America. Ken spent fifteen years working for Youth for Christ, and in the last twenty-five years he has traveled the nation as one of its top motivational and inspirational speakers. He has made appearances on television and on stages around the world and is the host of the popular daily radio show "Lighten Up!", heard on over five hundred stations across America. He provides a unique mixture of sidesplitting humor and heartwarming inspiration that never fails to delight and enrich audiences of all ages.

As president of Dynamic Communications, Ken offers seminars and a video series that teach speaking skills to ministry personnel and corporate executives. He has spoken to such groups as IBM, Focus on the Family, The Gaither Praise Gathering, AT&T, U.S. West, Youth Specialties, The Kellogg Corporation, and many more.

Ken was born and raised in the cold north country of Minnesota and is a graduate of Oak Hills Bible Institute in northern Minnesota. Ken and his wife, Diane, now live in Colorado. They have two daughters. Traci, their oldest, is married and lives in Colorado. Taryn is recently married and attends Belmont University in Tennessee. The entire family is involved in Ken's ministry, bringing much laughter and liberating truth to people around the world.

Ken is the author of eight books, some of which received national critical acclaim, including winning such prestigious awards as the Campus Life "Book of the Year" award and the Christian Bookseller's Association (CBA) Gold Medallion Award.

For more information on Ken Davis's workshops, training tools, personal appearances, calendar, and more, visit his website at **www.kendavis.com.**

LIGHTEN UP!
With Ken Davis

Ken Davis is the host of the popular radio show "Lighten Up!" Aired on over five hundred stations across America, this two-minute daily feature will brighten your day and encourage you in your walk with Jesus Christ. By means of his unique blend of humor and biblical insight, Ken Davis will challenge you to grow in your relationship to God, your family, and those around you.

To find out if "Lighten Up!" is aired in your city, call **303-470-5837** or visit **www.kendavis.com**

LIGHTEN UP! *also available on audiocassette*
Recorded before a live audience

LIGHTEN UP!
Great Stories from One of America's Favorite Storytellers

Ken Davis is a very funny guy. And as his friends and family will tell you, he's also a very wise one. After all, who but a wise guy would engineer some of the stunts Davis has pulled, then have the audacity to talk about them?

Like the time he shot a screwdriver through the ceiling of his kitchen with an M-80 firecracker? And who else would have an international collection of airline barf bags?

Only Ken Davis could narrate these stranger-than-life stories and use them to drive home insights that cut to the heart of Christlike living. Because Ken, being Ken, knows what human fallibility is all about. He knows how tough we adults can be on ourselves. He knows how hard we try to appear more together than we really are. And to all of us, he offers two words of very solid wisdom: LIGHTEN UP!

Ken's hilarious stories underscore one simple, encouraging theme: God's grace is for you. You're not perfect, but you are perfectly loved by God. So take heart. God doesn't just love you, he enjoys you. No reason you shouldn't too!

ISBN: 0-310-22974-X

Zondervan
AUDIO PAGES

Ken Davis

LIGHTEN UP!
Great stories from one of America's favorite storytellers

We want to hear from you. Please send your comments about this book
to us in care of the address below. Thank you.

ZondervanPublishingHouse
Grand Rapids, Michigan 49530
http://www.zondervan.com